To Barbara

Enjoy!

Patrick E. Murray

Bible Appreciation for Catholics

Learn the Bible. Love the Bible. Live the Bible.

Patrick Murray

WESTBOW
PRESS
A DIVISION OF THOMAS NELSON

WestBow Press books may be ordered through booksellers or by contacting:

WestBow Press
A Division of Thomas Nelson
1663 Liberty Drive
Bloomington, IN 47403
www.westbowpress.com
1-(866) 928-1240

ISBN: 978-1-4497-7623-7 (e)
ISBN: 978-1-4497-7624-4 (sc)
ISBN: 978-1-4497-7625-1 (hc)

Library of Congress Control Number: 2012921483
Printed in the United States of America
WestBow Press rev. date: 11/26/2012

Table Of Contents

Dedication

To all the people at St. Pius X Catholic Parish in Tucson, Arizona, an extraordinary Christian community, with warmth, openness, and loving leadership. Thank you. We miss you all.

Acknowledgments

The first I need to acknowledge and thank is my wife, Juliet, for her patience, her endless reading of drafts and revisions, her comments and advice both pros and cons, her suggestions of additional topics that readers would like to see, and who cheered me on when I thought I couldn't go further.

Many people in many different places over many years influenced me in my teaching about the Bible. I thank them all. In Tucson, Arizona, where I developed Bible appreciation, there are those who attended my Bible appreciation sessions. To them I owe many thanks. Their attention, active participation with their comments and questions, and encouragement ultimately led to writing this book. Of that group is Aurora Jimenez, who was my right hand, inviting, convincing, and registering friends and acquaintances to attend, and in general keeping things going year after year.

More immediately involved in getting the book completed is Patricia Goude, a friend and former co-worker, who masterfully edited and formatted the manuscript.

Lastly, I thank the people of WestBow Press, who have brought to fruition an idea and a dream.

Thank you all.

Patrick E. Murray
Colorado Springs, Colorado

About the Author

Patrick E. Murray has had a long association with the Bible. He studied twelve years of seminary education (religion, Latin, Greek, philosophy, Canon Law, Scripture, and theology) which brought him to ordination as a Catholic priest. In that profession he continued to study the Bible, preach biblical homilies, and teach Bible classes to high school students. After a number of years in priestly ministry, Murray requested and received a papal dispensation from his priestly responsibilities and pastoral ministry. Using his graduate degree in history, he entered a new profession as a field historian in the U.S. Air Force where he wrote histories of contemporary military operations and organization.

As a field historian, Murray and his family moved around--sometimes stateside, sometimes overseas. But at every location, he participated in the local parish. His favorite contribution involved adult Bible study and Bible classes. His longest assignment was ten years in Tucson, Arizona, and while he was there, he noticed a vacuum of knowledge or lack of interest in the Bible, so he created a unique introductory program in Bible awareness. He called it "Bible Appreciation," a one-of-a-kind beginner's class to open up the worlds of the Old Testament and the New Testament. The very successful Bible appreciation program integrated Bible classes with Murray's broad experience, history, theology, Latin and Greek, and catechism.

Murray and his wife, Juliet, live in Colorado Springs, Colorado. They enjoy traveling and spending time with their three children and two grandchildren.

Chapter I: Introduction

Welcome to *Bible Appreciation for Catholics*. This book has been written to invite everyone to learn about the Bible. The invitation is intended for everyone. *Bible Appreciation* is geared primarily for Catholics, but there are no restrictions for reading it. In fact, all Christians and non-Christians are invited to pick it up. Any motive for reading this book is fine, such as a desire to know more about the Bible, curiosity about the title of this book, checking it out for errors or fallacies, and trying to find out why anyone would want to be stuck in the mentality of a 2,500-year distant past.

This book presents a Catholic's view and understanding of the Holy Scriptures. It looks at what the Bible contains, how it was written, what the Catholic Church teaches about the Bible, why it is relevant in the twenty-first century, and what the Bible does for us.

Bible Appreciation for Catholics (or simply BA as you will find throughout the book) is not Bible study. The only relationship to Bible study is that it might create more interest so one may take up Bible study. But that is a personal decision for the person who has read this book. BA is not a scholarly study. It is a short, simple, and easy read designed to inform people how mature Catholics might benefit from learning more about the Bible.

Many Catholics do not see a need for reading the Bible. They are generally comfortable with their religious beliefs and practices. And, it is undeniable that Catholics can experience deep spiritual growth through the Eucharist, the other sacraments, personal prayer, and devotions. Notwithstanding the efficacy of traditional Catholic piety, it nevertheless fails to take advantage of the vast spiritual treasure at your fingertips. This book on Bible appreciation has come about as a result of teaching Catholic adults about the Bible. Whereas children and teens need to be taught the Bible according to their levels of understanding, Catholic adults who are not well acquainted with the Bible are short-changing their Christian maturity. Older Catholics may remember times when the Catholic Church did not emphasize personal Bible reading, but the official teaching of the Catholic Church since the Vatican II has been to encourage the laity to come to a greater appreciation and love of the sacred Scriptures through reading, studying, and praying.

Catholics are not ignorant of the Bible. Through regular weekly attendance at Mass, they receive a significant amount of Bible proclamation through the readings during the liturgy. The *Lectionary for Mass*, the book from which Bible passages are read at the Catholic eucharistic celebration, is divided into three yearly cycles: A, B, and C. Over a three-year period, a much broader presentation of Scripture readings is accomplished at Mass. So it is incorrect to say that Catholics do not know anything of the Bible, as some people claim. However, there is a major difference between hearing portions of the Bible read to the assembly and personally reading the Bible.

BA brings the Catholic into a personal familiarity with the Bible. Catholics believe the Bible is the Word of God and inspired by the Holy Spirit. This combination of faith beliefs, put into practice by regularly reading the Bible, can bring the Catholic to a new and deeper life in the Spirit. This results in a greater involvement in your personal relationship with the divine. It brings you closer to God.

■Is "Bible Appreciation" the Same as "Bible Study"?

That is a question frequently asked by people when they first encounter Bible appreciation. But as already stated, Bible appreciation is not the same as Bible study.

Bible appreciation is an introductory overview to the Holy Scriptures, which helps you understand why the Bible is such an awesome book and how you can most effectively read the Bible.

Bible study generally focuses on one particular book, such as the gospel of John. The Scripture study can go into this book looking at many aspects and from many different angles. It may examine the literal meaning of the narrative in light of the historical context. It might discover alternate meanings or nuances in interpretation because of a particular variation of the early Greek or Hebrew manuscripts. Such study may involve learning Hebrew, Aramaic, or Greek words and phrases, and how these may or may not enhance our understanding and interpretation of the particular scriptural passage involved.

It is easy to take an entire year to study the gospel of John. Bible study is fascinating, captivating, stimulating, and habit-forming. But, for the vast majority of Catholics, this is Scripture 401. For delving into the Bible, they need something they feel comfortable with. That is why we have Bible appreciation to decipher the hidden code and provide a password that allows access to understanding the Bible.

The Bible is a magnificent document. For many Catholics, it is an intimidating book to pick up and read. Some are embarrassed at how little they really know about the Bible. Many Catholics avoid encounters with people of other Christian denominations who visit their neighborhood offering pamphlets about the Bible and wishing to engage in discussion about it. Some Catholics shun Bible study groups because they don't want to show their ignorance of sacred Scripture, and some drop out of Bible study because they get lost in the details.

Such feelings or reactions are perfectly normal and understandable, in light of the many generations of Catholic families where the Bible was hardly touched other than to record basic family data. For hundreds of years, the Catholic Church did not encourage personal reading of the Bible. Catholics complied all too well. In our day and age, after centuries of disuse, Bible deficiency is probably genetic in Catholics!

Because we know so little about the Bible, it is awkward for us to plunge into Bible study sessions. Hopefully, BA will alleviate that awkward feeling. In college, we may take a course in music appreciation, or art appreciation, or even entomology appreciation, and we come away with a whole new vista of things that are so close and available to us. Until we engage a course in appreciation, we never realize what we have been missing!

■ The Goal of Bible Appreciation

The goal of *"Bible Appreciation"* is to increase awareness of the Bible and to learn Bible basics as far as what it consists of, how it was written, the historical context, the Catholic view and understanding, how the Bible fits into daily Catholic life, the liturgy, and our personal approach to spirituality.

When someone's awareness of the Bible is expanded, BA accomplishes its purpose. Bible study invites the "graduate" of Bible appreciation to take further study. When a person becomes comfortable with the Bible, then the Bible "sells itself."

So BA always begins with the basics, and it is not geared toward those who already know the basics. BA is an introductory survey of sacred Scripture. After reading a few segments of this book, you will feel quite comfortable opening the Bible. And, after reading this entire book you may become addicted to the Bible. And that will be absolutely marvelous, because the ultimate goal of Bible appreciation is reached in the 3 Ls: **learn** the Bible, **love** the Bible, and **live** the Bible.

Chapter II: Why Catholics Don't Read the Bible

There are many reasons why Catholics don't read the Bible. The reasons cover a broad spectrum and some are good and reasonable, but most are poor and unfortunate. Of the good reasons, many Catholics find spiritual meaning and comfort in their regular attendance at Mass, the other sacraments, praying the rosary, spiritual reading, prayer and faith-sharing groups, and participating in parish ministries. A poor reason is that Catholics do not perceive a need to read the Bible. I have asked Catholic relatives, friends, and acquaintances if they read the Bible and the vast majority answered that they do not.

Paul, a retired military veteran and a lifelong Catholic learned the importance and value of prayer when he was in Vietnam. When I asked Paul if he read the Bible, he answered, "No I don't; the Old Testament doesn't interest me at all. Now that I am retired, I am active in parish activities and I go to Mass every day. For me, the holy Eucharist is the most sublime thing there is. Receiving the body and blood of Jesus gives me the strength to get through the day and live my life as Jesus teaches us."

Jeanette is a widow and lives by herself. She was baptized and raised as a Catholic. The family lived in the same parish, and the parish priest did not teach anything about reading the Bible. When Jeanette got married, she took a one-year Bible study class. I asked if she read the Bible as a daily devotion. She answered, "I stopped reading the Bible after taking that Bible study course, but I do like the monthly booklet *Our Daily Bread* that has Bible passages and brief prayers and meditations. With that, I feel the presence of the Holy Spirit; in my heart I can do all my praying to the Lord."

Robert is a successful businessman and has a good Catholic family. I asked him if regular Bible reading was part of his Catholicism. He answered, "No, I don't read the Bible because I don't get out anything worthwhile. I did read the entire Bible once, but I haven't read the Bible since then. The message is antiquated and offers little to the modern world."

Occasionally, I come across the Catholic who grew up in a non-Bible-reading Catholic home, yet reads the Bible now. "I was brought up by two women who were devout Catholics and followed the beliefs of the Church. They went to Mass and listened to the Gospels and obeyed the messages the priest gave through preaching. I never saw a Bible in the house. What they taught me was that the Bible was only for Protestants. In history classes at school I learned some things about the Bible like the first book printed by Gutenberg was the Bible, and that the Bible was a collection of many small books, and that Martin Luther rebelled against the Catholic Church. His rebelling led to the Protestant Reformation and the Protestant Bible. When I was 18, I began to study the Bible. Since then, I've been reading the Bible all my life."

■ Historical Reasons

For the past 400-plus years, the Catholic laity traditionally has had many non-Bible readers. When we look at why Catholics don't read the Bible many factors are involved. This custom has its roots in events that transpired almost 500 years ago when Martin Luther posted his famous

95 Theses on the church door in Wittenberg, Germany. But the blame for non-Bible reading Catholics cannot simply be put on Luther. The reason is far more complex.

To understand, let's step back in history. Christians have been hungry for the Holy Scriptures since the beginning of Christianity. At first, Christians collected bits and pieces. Maybe a collection of the epistles of St. Paul. Maybe some Christians wanted a copy of St. Mark's gospel. Perhaps they acquired copies of the four Gospels and bound them in codices. As time went on and Christianity spread to the known world, Greek ceased to be the dominant language. In the Roman Empire, Latin was the language of the people. And, in time, copies of the Bible were made in Latin. In the Eastern frontiers of Christianity, sacred Scriptures were translated into Coptic, Syriac, Ethiopic, and other vernaculars that the common people could understand. In the Western world after the fall of the Roman Empire, Latin ceased to be the dominant language. In the thirteenth, fourteenth and fifteenth centuries, Bibles were translated into English, German, French, and other European languages.

Also at this time, the Catholic Church was rich and powerful in the social and political world. The state of the Catholic Church was immersed in moral decline and tremendous corruption. Nepotism was rampant. The pope and bishops appointed anyone to high ecclesiastical posts, regardless of their age, qualifications, and moral rectitude. Another aspect of the Catholic hierarchy was their lavish and reckless lifestyle, a sad example for the faithful. Another practice was giving dispensations for a good price.

The most repugnant and despised corrupt practice was the selling of indulgences. An indulgence was a religious practice that one could earn points so to speak that would save one's soul from temporal punishment due to sins. If you had done something wrong, you could make it up by doing penance or acts of charity, making a pilgrimage, giving alms, or performing some other good deed. This was a way to encourage Christians to lead a decent life. The concept of indulgences was very old in the church, starting in the second or third century. The difference between the third century and the sixteenth century was that the early years did not sell indulgences. But in the fifteenth and sixteenth centuries the Catholic Church found a way to make more money by selling years of repealed punishment if the penitent paid the right amount of money. This practice was one of the main causes in the Protestant revolt. Selling indulgences was scandalous and needed to be stopped.

The sixteenth century in Europe was a mess. Problems and turmoil plagued all levels and areas of society: in the Church, in political issues, in social upheaval, and in economic changes. In addition to the corrupt practices mentioned above, the political upheaval was tremendous. The influence of the Church in political affairs was weakening. Respect for the Church's spiritual authority was eroding.

Luther's thesis was in protest against a number of practices in the Catholic Church. The most noticeable practice was selling indulgences. Luther did not plan to cause an irreparable break in Christianity; he was protesting the corruption that he saw in the Catholic Church especially with the hierarchy. The hierarchy struck back. Nevertheless, the breakup of Christianity did happen.

The Protestant Reformation discarded many practices of the Catholic Church. A significant change the reformers made was to the Christian Bible. The Catholic Church officially recognized the Latin version of the Bible, which was based on the Greek language version known as the Septuagint, but the reformers rejected this Bible and accepted only the Hebrew language Bible as the only authentic Bible. There were more books in the Septuagint than in the Hebrew Bible, which is reflected in the differences you have today between the Catholic Bible and the

Protestant Bible. You will see more about this later in the discussion on the "canon" of the Bible.

In response to the Protestant reformation, the Catholic Church convened the Council of Trent (1545–1563). One of the numerous declarations on Catholic dogma dealt with the Bible. Part of this declaration stated forcibly that "No one is permitted to interpret sacred Scripture contrary to this sense nor contrary to the unanimous consent of the fathers." Regarding the correct number and list of books in the Bible, the council fathers stated, "If anyone does not accept these books as sacred and canonical in their entirety, with all their parts, according to the text usually read in the Catholic Church and as they are in the ancient Latin Vulgate, but knowingly and willfully contemns the traditions previously mentioned: let him be anathema."

> "To keep undisciplined minds under proper control, the Council decrees that no one should dare to rely on his own judgment in matters of faith and morals affecting the structure of Christian doctrine and to distort sacred Scripture to fit meanings of his own that are contrary to the meaning that holy mother church has held and now holds; for it is her office to judge about the true sense and interpretation of the sacred Scripture."
>
> [*The Church Teaches*, Clarkson, Edwards, Kelly, and Welch, 1955]

The Council of Trent did not forbid private Bible reading, but it had pronounced enough dogmatic statements to deter the laity from doing so. As a result, personal reading of the Bible by the laity began to diminish and other spiritual practices became the norm.

Another source of contention between Catholicism and Protestantism fueled the dispute. A principal doctrine in the Catholic Church is that divine revelation comes from two sources: the Scriptures and tradition.

Catholic tradition is "the present manifestation of the revealed truth that the church's teaching authority holds fresh in its consciousness." Tradition is the Church's teaching of the revelation made by Christ and the spirit to the apostles. On the other side, Protestants maintained that personal interpretation of sacred Scripture was a sufficient rule of faith. There was no need for a church to explain revelation to the faithful. As such, the slogan of the reformers, *"sola scriptura"* (only scripture), was the only necessity for understanding and interpreting the Bible. With sola scriptura, the Protestant churches took over the Bible, and the Catholic laity relinquished the Bible.

With the Protestant Reformation and the Catholic Counter-Reformation, neither side acted like Christians. They were not exemplars of "they will know you by your love." The animosity between the two was horrendous. Where the kings and queens were Catholic, they could kill Protestants. Where the kings and queens were Protestant, they could kill the Catholics. Such royal leadership led the laity to despise the opposite side and distance themselves as far as possible from the religious customs of the opposition. Catholics kept their prayers and statues of saints, the Protestants kept the Bible. The Catholics prayed their rosary; the Protestants scorned them and read their Bibles.

For the following 400 years, even though the Catholic Church leadership did not forbid laity to read the Bible, the pastoral emphasis was on the Mass, sacraments, and traditional devotions.

■ Traditional Catholic Spirituality

Significant changes in traditional Catholic spirituality have occurred since the Second Vatican Council (Vatican II). After two generations, younger Catholics are leaving some of the old traditions behind. Nevertheless, the traditional Catholic spirituality and devotions are still alive. Traditional Catholic spirituality focused on: (1) mass and the seven sacraments, (2) rosary and devotions, and (3) corporal or spiritual works of mercy.

■ The Power of the Eucharist

Since the celebration of the Eucharist in the vernacular was allowed by Vatican II, Catholics have a greater participation and attention at Mass. When the Mass was in Latin, it was not uncommon to see devout Catholics praying the rosary during Mass because the altar was farther away from the congregation and the priest had his back to the congregation while reciting Latin prayers in a nearly inaudible mumble. When the priest turned around to say "*Dominus vobiscum*," the altar boys responded "*et cum spiritu tuo*" for the people. Theologically, Mass was more spiritually efficacious; personally, the rosary was more spiritually satisfying. Today, you seldom see this custom.

The Holy Eucharist has always been the heart of Catholic faith and the essence of its understanding of what it means to be church. The Eucharist is a great mystery of faith. As is the incarnation, God made man. The passion, death, and resurrection of Jesus Christ is the supreme act of redemption by the Son of God, the Second Person of the Divine Trinity, the overwhelming and incomprehensible act of love for all creation and obedient submission to the Father. Meditating and contemplating the cross is more than enough to satisfy the hungriest of hearts and the soul's search for spiritual meaning. Actually receiving the bread of life is the most sublime act a human can do. We participate in the act of the redemption of the world. We stand before the cross. We share in the Last Supper. We're offered new life. The general understanding and appreciation of the Eucharist varies greatly. But, even a modest or elementary appreciation, together with devout reception of communion, can certainly justify a Catholic's assumption that one does not need to read the Bible.

■Religious Traditions versus Bible Reading

Catholic religious traditions were well entrenched for several hundred years. An old book (something of a catechism) I bought in a book store specializing in antiquated volumes illustrates the fact that the Catholic Church did not encourage the laity to read the Bible. This book, written by Msgr. William Byrne in 1892, presents a picture of what a devout Catholic should do to save his or her soul. This book is divided into three parts: Part I deals with the chief truths of religion, Part II deals with the moral law, and Part III looks at the "Means of Salvation." This last part of the book offers detailed lessons on Catholic spirituality, and a spirituality which has endured 120 years, and will continue on because it is true and it works. Whether every Catholic practices it or not, it is familiar to all Catholics.

[*Catholic Doctrine*, Wm.Bryne, Boston, 1892]

The Means to Salvation in Part III begins explaining that "grace is a supernatural gift freely bestowed on us by God for our eternal salvation." There are two basic kinds of grace: sanctifying and actual. Sanctifying grace is "a divine gift infused into the soul and abiding therein as a habit, whereby we are justified and holy and pleasing in the sight of God." Actual grace is that "gift of God that helps us to do well and avoid evil. It is called actual because it is the active influence of the Holy Spirit enlightening the mind and moving the will to each good deed."

After the brief explanation of what is sanctifying grace and actual grace, the author teaches that prayer is "the most ordinary means of grace and is within the reach of all, at all times." The recommended prayers are the Our Father, Hail Mary, Apostles' Creed, Confiteor, and Act of Contrition. The mass and the sacraments are the next. Then, there are many other devotions, and religious practices such as Stations of the

Cross, Exposition of the Blessed Sacrament, and Benediction. Catholics are accustomed to sacramentals such as wearing blessed medals and scapulars, making the sign of the cross frequently, venerating relics of saints, and lighting devotional candles. In Catholic homes, crucifixes and statues, pictures of Jesus, Mary, and different saints, are common reminders of the love of God and love of one's neighbor.

All of these things have been going on among the Catholic laity for several hundred years, and in Catholic families, many of the personal preferences have been handed down from generation to generation. So, this is why many Catholics do not feel they have a need to read the Bible.

Reinforcing the custom that Catholics don't need to read the Bible, the spiritual guidance offered in Byrne's book is that personal reading of the Bible is not mentioned one time in 450 pages.

✟

Chapter III: The Bible Appreciation First Step

■ Open the Bible

The Bible, which is still a mystery for many Catholics, will remain a mystery unless the first step is taken to simply pick up the Bible and open it. The best way to read *Bible Appreciation for Catholics* is to have a Bible close at hand.

As we have it today, and as it has been for centuries, the Bible is what we call a book. It is a rectangular block of pages of paper with either a hard cover or a soft cover. It may be bound with leather with gilt edge pages, or a clothbound hardback, or even a paperback. But it is definitely recognizable as a book.

The name "Bible" comes from the Greek word (and later, Latin) *Biblia*, which means "books." We know what a book looks like, and we don't have to be told that the Bible is a book. However, the point that the Bible is easily recognized as a book is precisely one of the ways the Bible may be a mystery, or an object of intimidation, or confusion, or misconceptions.

The Bible has not always been a book. It did not start out as a book. For many centuries it was not written in any fashion. When the first parts of it were written (sometime between 800–600 B.C.), it was not written in anything that resembled a book or fit any of our mental images of a book. Holy Scriptures were written on scrolls.

Now, open your Bible to the first book, Genesis, and find the beginning of the story of Abram. It is not necessary to read the chapters at this time. Just skip through the main episodes and see what and where they are.

You will notice that all the parts of the Bible have numbered chapters and numbered verses, something like "Genesis Chapter 12, verses 1–3," God's call to Abram. The chapter and verse numbers make it easy to locate particular parts of the Bible. Of course, when the Bible was written, nothing had numbered chapters and verses. The introduction of chapters and verses in Bibles developed over several hundred years. Early in the thirteenth century, Stephen Langton, the Archbishop of Canterbury, divided the Bible into chapters. Two hundred years later, Rabbi Isaac Nathan divided the Old Testament into numbered verses, and Robert Estienne, a Frenchman, did the same with the New Testament in 1551.

There are several ways a chapter/verse is written. For example, the first line in the book of Genesis could be abbreviated as Gen 1:1 or Gen 1/1. If you wanted to identify more than just one verse, like where to find the eight beatitudes, it would be Mt 5:1–10 or Mt 5/1–10. In this case, the "Mt" is the abbreviation of Matthew. You will find some variety in the designations, depending on what version of the Bible you have. There is no strict universal method of abbreviating names of the books. Every Bible usually has a list of the abbreviations in the first few pages. Genesis might be "Gen" or "Gn," Numbers might be "Num" or "Nb." It might seem a bit complicated at first, but it will soon be second nature.

Before proceeding further, you might want to take a short Bible quiz that follows. The purpose of the quiz is for your own self-evaluation.

Perhaps you know all the answers; perhaps you can only answer two or three. That is immaterial at this time, but after you finish *Bible Appreciation,* you will be fully able to answer these questions.

Patrick Murray

Bible Appreciation Quiz for Chapter III

What do you know about the Bible?

Write your answers on the line below the question.

(1.) How many books are in the Bible? 42, 66, 72, 84, 109? (Actually, this is a tricky question!)

_____

(2.) Who were Adam and Eve's two sons?

_____

(3.) Name the four Gospels.

_____

(4.) What is the first book of the Bible?

_____

(5.) Was Abraham's wife turned into a pillar of salt?

_____

(6.) King David was the father of which Israelite king?

_____

(7.) What book of the Bible records the events of Moses bringing the Israelites out of Egypt?

_____

(8.) Which of the following is not a book of the Bible? Joshua, Isaiah, Moses, Daniel, Numbers.

_____

(9.) Abraham lived about 1900 B.C. Calculating the genealogies according to the Bible, when did Adam live? 500 B.C.; 4000 B.C.; 10,000 B.C.; 20,000 B.C.

_____

(10.) What is the last book of the Bible?

_____

(11.) What is the Pentateuch?

_____

(12.) How many epistles of St. Peter are there in the Bible?

_____

(13.) Name the four major prophets of the Old Testament.

_____

(14.) Name three Judges of the Old Testament.

_____

(15.) What is Bible "pre-history" and where do you find it?

_____

(16.) Where in the Bible do we find the names of the twelve apostles?

_____

You can check your answers in Appendix A.

How well did you do? Make a note of your answers. You will not be given the answers yet, but well before the end of this book you will know all these questions and very much more.

■ Time to open up the Bible

Now, open the Bible you have close at hand. You will find in the first pages a table of contents and a list of the "Books of the Bible," or "The Books of the Old and New Testaments." At the very outset, the reader finds out that the Bible is a book of many other books. That is not a misrepresentation. It **is** a book of many individual books, written by many writers, over a very long period of time, (even longer than the number of years Methuselah lived, which the Bible says was 967). This fact of there being many books in the Bible is important, and one that will have a major role in Bible appreciation and any further investigations in the Bible you may choose to undertake later on.

In some Bibles, the list of books is in alphabetical order beginning with the book of Acts and ending with the book of Zephaniah. This list is not in the order that the books appear in the Bible. As they appear in the Bible, the first book is the book of Genesis. Genesis means beginning, and the story of this book begins back before time began. If you count the number of books in the Old Testament, beginning with Genesis, you may find a list of thirty-nine books, or a list of forty-six. If the list has thirty-nine books, then the Bible you have is the traditional Protestant Bible. If it has forty-six books, then it is the traditional Catholic Bible. The latter number could also mean that the Bible you have is modern Protestant edition or translation that contains a larger collection of books than the older traditional Protestant Bible.

[The explanation of these differences is found in the segment of this book titled "Catholic Bibles and Protestant Bibles," and also in the segment titled "Apocrypha."]

After the list of books of the Old Testament, you will find the list of the twenty-seven books of the New Testament. It is the same for Protestant and Catholic Bibles. The following comparison provides a quick look at the difference between the Catholic and Protestant bibles.

■ Catholic Bibles and Protestant Bibles

[Note again: This compares the traditional Catholic Bible (forty-six books) and the traditional Protestant Bible (thirty-nine books).]

Old Testament

Catholic Bible	Protestant Bible
Genesis	Genesis
Exodus	Exodus
Leviticus	Leviticus
Numbers	Numbers
Deuteronomy	Deuteronomy
Joshua	Joshua
Judges	Judges
Ruth	Ruth
1 Samuel (1 Kings*)	1 Samuel
2 Samuel (2 Kings*)	2 Samuel
1 Kings (3 Kings*)	1 Kings
2 Kings (4 Kings*)	2 Kings
1 Chronicles (1 Paralipomena*)	1 Chronicles
2 Chronicles (2 Paralipomena*)	2 Chronicles
Ezra (Esdras*)	Ezra
Nehemiah (Nehemiah*)	Nehemiah
Tobit (Tobias*)	--
Judith	--
Esther	Esther
Job	Job
Psalms	Psalms
Proverbs	Proverbs
Ecclesiastes	Ecclesiastes
Song of Songs (Canticle of Canticles*)	Song of Songs

Old Testament

Catholic Bible	Protestant Bible
Wisdom	--
Sirach (Ecclesiasticus*)	--
Isaiah (Isaias*)	Isaiah
Jeremiah (Jeremias*)	Jeremiah
Lamentations	Lamentations
Baruch	--
Ezekiel (Ezechkiel*)	Ezekiel
Daniel	Daniel
Hosea (Osee*)	Hosea
Joel	Joel
Amos	Amos
Obadiah (Abdias*)	Obadiah
Jonah (Jonas*)	Jonah
Micah (Michaeas*)	Micah
Nahum	Nahum
Habakkuk (Habacuc*)	Habakkuk
Zephaniah (Sophonias*)	Zephaniah
Haggai (Aggaeus*)	Haggai
Zechariah (Zacharias*)	Zechariah
Malachi (Malachias*)	Malachi
1 Maccabees (1 Machabees*)	--
2 Maccabees (2 Machabees*)	--

* [The asterisk indicates the names of the books as found in the Latin translation of the Bible. In the last 50–60 years, there has been major cooperation between the Roman Catholic Church and the main stream Protestant Churches in Old Testament biblical scholarship. The Hebrew spelling is now found in Catholic bibles.]

New Testament

(Twenty-seven books, same for both Catholic and

Protestant bibles)

Matthew

Mark

Luke

John

Acts of the Apostles

Romans

1 Corinthians

2 Corinthians

Galatians

Ephesians

Philippians

Colossians

1 Thessalonians

2 Thessalonians

1 Timothy

2 Timothy

Titus

Philemon

Hebrews

James

1 Peter

2 Peter

1 John

2 John

3 John

Jude

Revelation (Apocalypse)

The books of the Old Testament originated in the Holy Scriptures of the Hebrews, or Jewish people, whereas, the New Testament books originated in the writings of Christians in the first century. Together, the Old Testament and the New Testament make up the Christian Bible.

Now, flip through the pages of your Bible beginning with the book of Genesis and go all the way through the Old Testament, making special note of the books that follow. After Genesis is Exodus, after Exodus is Leviticus, and so on. After you reach the end of this list, regardless of the name of the final book, do the same with the list of books of the New Testament.

Once you have made this important step of opening the Bible and perusing the books in the Old and New Testaments, the Bible appreciation phases can begin.

The approach we take for learning about the Bible in BA is historical and chronological. As your knowledge and familiarity of the Bible grow, other approaches may be more appropriate. But in BA, the historical and chronological approach seems to be the easiest road to follow. Our modern minds are well-tuned to recognize the sequence of historical events, and a chronological presentation of things that happen is something we can more readily associate with. Moreover, the Bible is historical in nature, although there is so much more in it than simply historical facts and episodes. A later segment in this book "Interpretation of the Bible" will enter into different levels of understanding the Bible.

Chapter IV:
Understanding and Reading the Old Testament

▪ Preliminary Considerations about the Bible

The Bible has two basic divisions, which are determined by the relation to the birth of Jesus Christ: the Old and New Testaments. The Old Testament records the special communication of God with humankind before the birth of Christ. The New Testament records the special communication of God with humankind after the birth of Christ.

The Bible is a book, but it is not "a" book. By this, I mean that the Bible in its human production was not written by one individual. It is a collection or a compilation of a number of books written and revised by a number of people over many years. The human element in the writing of the Bible is a source of controversy among some Christians. As a collection of different writings, each "testament" is comparable to any small library a person might have.

That is…

> …(1) some parts report events,
>
> …(2) some parts express opinion,
>
> …(3) some parts entertain,
>
> …(4) some parts edify,
>
> …(5) some parts inspire, and
>
> …(6) some parts instruct.

Both the Old Testament and the New Testament can be divided into three groups of writings (a traditional approach):

> (1) historical books: records events, lives, and times;
>
> (2) prophetical books: the teachings and preaching of selected personalities; and
>
> (3) wisdom books: advice and counsel on how to live properly.

■ Old Testament

The Old Testament is exactly what its title implies. It is the old message, the older revelations God made to man. The adjective "old" is not to be interpreted as venerable or of more value or anything like that. It is old because it preceded the later testament in time. The term "testament" can be taken to mean witness and covenant. Thus, the Old Testament is the previous witness and earlier covenant. This description provides a valuable distinction for understanding God's communication to man. For Catholics, it is of paramount importance. The term Old Testament is a name coined in the early years of the Christian era. The Hebrew Bible does not use the term Old Testament because it does not have the New Testament.

■New Testament

The New Testament is new not only because it is the more recent of the two testaments. The New Testament is a new witness and a new covenant between God and man, accomplished totally in the existence of the God-man, Jesus Christ. The New Testament is new because it completely replaces the Old Testament in terms of God's revelation and relationship with creation. This is not meant to imply that the Old Testament has little value for those who believe in Jesus Christ. The Old Testament is valuable precisely because it is the inspired word of God, and it has a very human element that resonates deeply within the heart, soul, and conscience of every man. We can see mirror images of ourselves in many of the people and episodes in the Old Testament. The more we read the Old Testament, the more it will make sense, and, the more the New Testament will make an impact on our lives.

■Reading the Old Testament

A general sense of history helps when you read the Old Testament. The period of the Old Testament covers about 1700 years from the life and times of Abraham (ca. 1800 B.C.) to the family of Judas Maccabeus (ca. 150 B.C.). Notice that the two books of the Maccabees are not included in the Hebrew Bible (also known as the Palestine Canon). For the Jews, divine revelation ended between 500 and 400 B.C. The book of Ezra and Nehemiah was the last book in the Hebrew Bible that was written in Hebrew.

Time Period	Historical Books	Prophets/Wisdom
?	Genesis 1–11	I
1800 B.C.	Genesis 12–50	I
1300 B.C.	Exodus Numbers Leviticus Deuteronomy	I
1200 B.C.	Joshua Judges Ruth	I
1000 B.C.	1 Samuel 2 Samuel	I
750 B.C.	1 Kings	Isaiah, Jeremiah Ezekiel, Daniel, Hosea, Joel, Amos
712 B.C.	2 Kings 1 Chronicles 2 Chronicles	Obediah, Jonah, Micah, Nahum, Habakuk , Zeferiah, Haggai, Zechariah, Malachi
580 B.C.	Job, Psalms, Proverbs, Ecclesiastes, Judith, Tobit, Esther, Sirach, Wisdom, Song of Songs	I
450 B.C.	Ezra Nehemiah	I

| **200 B.C.** | 1 Maccabees | I |
| | 2 Maccabees | |

Birth of Christ

■ One Way to Read the Old Testament

In BA we don't get into an in-depth reading of the Bible at any time. The first objectives of BA are getting familiar with content of the Bible and becoming comfortable navigating through it. When you do get around to reading the Old Testament for the first time, I suggest reading it in a way that is more in tune with the modern mind. This is the historical, chronological approach. It follows the familiar Bible stories we've heard since we were children. It helps you get familiar with the different stories and where they are in the Bible. In reading the Old Testament:

…..first, read the historical accounts

…..second, read the prophets

…..third, read the wisdom books.

The **Historical Books** of the Old Testament are presented as more or less chronological accounts covering about 1,400 years from the time of Abraham (ca. 1800 B.C.) up to the return of the Hebrews from the Babylonian Exile and the subsequent rebuilding of Jerusalem and the temple under Ezra and Nehemiah (ca. 450 B.C.). One of the differences between Catholic bibles and Protestant bibles is found here. Catholic bibles have historical books that extend the history of the Jewish people up to about 150 B.C. These are the two books of the Maccabees, found in Catholic bibles, but not in older Protestant bibles. This explanation is discussed in the section of this book on "deuterocanonical" books and "Apocrypha." There are sixteen or eighteen books in the historical grouping (again depending on whether you are using a Catholic bible or a Protestant bible).

In what follows, you will note that I suggest skipping certain books or parts of books. This because a lot of detail about laws, descriptions about the Hebrew campsite, priestly garments, and other details are not particularly interesting the first time you read the Bible.

(1) *Genesis* – Read all chapters. Traces the history of Israel from its beginning with God's promise to Abraham, then Isaac, Jacob, and Joseph.

(2) *Exodus* – Read chapters 1–20 and chapter 40 about Moses in Exodus, Israel's escape from slavery and oppression, the Ten Commandments, the Ark of the Covenant, the tabernacle, and the Hebrew priesthood. Skip chapters 21–39 that interrupt the flow of historical events.

(3) *Leviticus* – Skip this entire book the first time you read the Bible.

(4) *Numbers* – Read chapters 1–4 and 9–14 about the trek through the desert. Skip chapters 5– 8, 15–19, and 20–36. Not a very inspirational book. A lot of laws and regulations covering sacrifices, offerings, rules concerning the clean and unclean, and sexual impurities.

(5) *Deuteronomy* – Read chapters 31–34 about the last days of Moses. Skip chapters 1–30 the first time you read Deuteronomy.

(6) *Joshua* – Read all chapters about the conquest of the promised land.

(7) *Judges* – Read all chapters – A period of 100+ years when Israel had different leaders before the monarchy was

established. [Samson, Gideon, Deborah, etc.]

(8) *1 Samuel* – Read all chapters – Samuel and the creation of the monarchy and the kingdom.

(9) *2 Samuel* – Read all chapters – The lives of King Saul and King David.

(10) *1 Kings* – Read all chapters – The life of King Solomon and the division of the kingdom after his death.

(11) *2 Kings* – Read all chapters – The story of the divided kingdom: Israel in the North and Judah in the south. This ends with the Babylonian Exile.

(12) *1 Chronicles and 2 Chronicles*. **Skip** these books the first time you read the Bible. They mostly repeat the books of 1 and 2 Kings and tribal genealogies.

(13) *Ezra* – Read all chapters – The return from Exile and the revival of the Jewish nation and religious fidelity to God.

(14) *Nehemiah* – Read all chapters – Rebuilding the nation and the Temple.

(15) *1 Maccabees* – Read all chapters – The Jewish revolt.

(16) *2 Maccabees* – Read all chapters – More stories about the Jewish revolt.

■ Brief Overview of the Pentateuch

The Pentateuch is the first five books of the Old Testament: Genesis, Exodus, Leviticus, Numbers, and Deuteronomy. In this overview, we take a cursory look at the five books to get some idea of their content.

So open your Bible, beginning with…yes, Genesis. Look for the group and sequence of the books in the Pentateuch.

Genesis	Pre-history	Chapters 1–11
(ca. 1800 B.C)	Abraham	Chapters 12–25
	Isaac and Jacob	Chapters 26–36
(ca.1500 B.C.)	Joseph	Chapters 37–50
Exodus	Liberation from Egypt	Chapter 1–15:21
(ca. 1300. B.C.	Journey through Desert	Chapter 15:22–18
	Covenant at Sinai	Chapters 19–24
	Instruction on Building the Sanctuary and its Ministries	Chapters 25–31
	The Golden Calf and Renewal of the Covenant	Chapters 32–40
Leviticus	Ritual of Sacrifice	Chapters 1–8
	Investiture of Priests	Chapters 8–10
	Rules of Clean and Unclean	Chapters 11–16
	Law of Holiness	Chapters 17–26
	Tariffs	Chapter 27

Numbers	Census	Chapters 1–4
	Various Laws	Chapters 5–6
	Offerings of Leaders and Consecration of Levites	Chapters 7–8
	Keeping the Passover	Chapters 9–10
	Halts in the Desert	Chapters 11–14
	Sacrifices and the Power of Priests	Chapters 15–19
	Kadesh to Moab	Chapters 20–25
	More Laws	Chapters 31–34
	Spoils of War	Chapters 31–34
	On the Plains of Moab	Chapters 35–36
Deuteronomy	1st Discourse of Moses	Chapters 1–4
	2nd Discourse of Moses	Chapters 4–11
	Deuteronomic Code (Second Law)	Chapters 12–26
	Concluding Discourses	Chapters 26–30
	Last Actions and Death of Moses	Chapters 31–34

From a historical perspective, the Jewish people experienced three major events. The Exodus and the years in the desert that followed was the most significant event in the history of Israel. The next major event in Israel's history was the Babylonian exile when the people were deported to Babylon and the city of Jerusalem was totally destroyed. The third major significant event in the history of the Jewish people was the return from exile and freedom in their homeland.

■ Overview of Historical Books of Pre-Exilic Period (1200–586 B.C.)

The historical books of the pre-exilic period are Joshua, Judges, Ruth, 1 and 2 Samuel, 1 and 2 Kings, and 1 and 2 Chronicles. As we did in our quick trip through the Pentateuch, we will do the same for the pre-exilic period.

Joshua (ca. 1200 B.C.)	Crossing the Jordan River and Battle of Jericho	Chapters 1–6
	Conquest of the Land of Canaan	Chapters 7–12
	Division of the land among the Tribes of Israel	Chapters13–23
	Joshua Confirms the Covenant	Chapter 24

Judges (ca. 1100 B.C.)	Introduction -- Lives and adventures of the Judges: Othniel, Ehud, Shamgar, Deborah, Gideon, Jephthah, several minor	Chapters 1–2
	Judges, Samson	Chapters 2–16
	Two other episodes	Chapters 17–2
Ruth (ca. 1100 B.C.)	Great-grandmother of David	Chapters 1–4
1 Samuel (ca. 1000 B.C.)	Life of Samuel	Chapters 1–8
	Saul as King	Chapters 9–15
	David and Saul	Chapters 16–31
2 Samuel	David, King of Judah and Israel	Chapters 5–24
1 Kings (ca. 900 B.C.)	Death of King David	Chapters 1–2
	King Solomon	Chapters 2–11
	The Divided Kingdom	Chapters 12–22
2 Kings (800–600 B.C.)	Kings of Judah and Israel until the end of the Kingdom of Israel	Chapters 1–17
	Kings of Judah up to the fall of Jerusalem	Chapters 17–25

1 Chronicles (ca. 1000 B.C.)	Genealogies of the Hebrew People	Chapters 1–9
	King David, the Great Monarch	Chapters 10–22
	David makes Solomon his successor	Chapters 23–29
2 Chronicles (ca.900-600 B.C.)	Kingship of Solomon	Chapters 1–10
	King Rehoboam and King Jeroboam	Chapters 11–12
	Struggles of the divided Kingdom	Chapters 13–35
	Babylonian Exile	Chapter 36

■ Overview of Historical Books of Post-Exilic Period (500–180 B.C.)

The books of the post-exilic period are Ezra, Nehemiah, Tobit, Judith, Esther, 1 and 2 Maccabees. Follow the same procedures as we mentioned before.

Ezra (ca. 500 B.C.)	Hebrews return from exile in Babylon	Chapters 1–6
	Deeds of Ezra: the reconstruction of Jerusalem and building the Second Temple	Chapters 7-10
Nehemiah (ca. 450 B.C.)	Governor of Judah	Chapters 1–7
	Deeds of Nehemiah	Chapters 8–13

This is the end of the books listed in the Palestine Canon of the Hebrew-speaking Jews. The books of Tobit, Judith, Esther, and 1 and 2 Maccabees which follow the book of Nehemiah in the Catholic Bible, were listed in the Alexandrine Canon of the Greek-speaking Jews. The books of Tobit, Judith, and Esther are considered more as inspirational religious-historical novels, rather than factual events.

Tobit (ca. 400 B.C.)	A story about Tobit and his son Tobias	Chapters 1–14
Judith (?-------?B.C.)	A courageous Hebrew woman when Israel was attacked	Chapters 1–13
Esther (Exile period)	A Hebrew woman becomes queen and saves her people	Chapters 5–24

I Maccabees (ca. 180 B.C.)	Introduction and Maccabean Revolt	Chapters 1–2
	Leadership of Judas Maccabeus	Chapters 3–9
	Leadership of Jonah Maccabeus	Chapters 10–12
	Leadership of Simon Maccabeus	Chapters 13–16
II Maccabees (ca. 180 B.C.)	Introduction: Letter to the Jews in Egypt	Chapters 1–2
	Profanation of the Temple and Persecution of the Jews	Chapters 3–7
	Victories of Judas Maccabeus	Chapters 8–10
	Renewed Persecution of the Jews	Chapters 10–15

The Prophets in the Bible

The term "prophet" in our everyday language usually refers to someone who predicts the future. When we are accustomed to such a meaning, we can easily miss the message and impact of the various books of the prophets in the Old Testament. Whereas, we do see some prophecy and prediction in the Old Testament prophetical writings; the main point we need to recognize is that prophets are the spokespersons of God. The prophet's primary role is to speak God's message to the people. As a result, many of the prophetical writings speak of God's fidelity to his people, his abiding presence, his tender care, his constant love, his protection, and his bountiful providence. And seen in its entirety, this is the real message of Divine Revelation.

The prophetic messages may be cast in numerous ways: reminders to the people about their history and heritage; threats and warnings about their infidelity to God. In getting their prophetical messages across to the people, the prophets used stories, examples, actions that illustrate a point, and visions.

There were many prophets in Old Testament times. Some wrote and some did not. The group of books we call the prophets are from the writing prophets. As seen earlier, there are sixteen writing prophets. The four most famous and easily remembered are Isaiah, Jeremiah, Ezekiel, and Daniel.[1] These are also referred to as the major prophets. Twelve other prophets are referred to as the minor prophets. The terms major prophets and minor prophets are determined by the size of their books, not by some hierarchical importance. The minor prophets are in the order they appear in the Bible: (1) Hosea, (2) Joel, (3) Amos, (4) Obadiah, (5) Jonah, (6) Micah, (7) Nahum, (8) Habakkuk, (9) Zephaniah, (10) Haggai, (11) Zechariah, and (12) Malachi. The four major prophets and twelve minor prophets lived and preached some time between 800 and 500 B.C.

---

1   Due to recent research and biblical criticism, some biblical scholars do not rank
     Daniel with the three other major prophets.

Major Prophets	**Minor Prophets**
Isaiah	Hosea, Joel,
Jeremiah	Obadiah, Amos,
Ezekiel	Michah, Jonah,
Daniel	Nahum, Habakuk, Zeferiah, Haggai, Zechariah, Malachi

The prophets lived and wrote during the times of the Kings of Judah and Israel up to the time of captivity and exile. Read the prophetical books after reading the historical books, because you will have a better feel for the historical context of their times. You might want to refer back and forth between the prophets and

.... 1 and 2 Samuel
.... 1 and 2 Kings
.... 1 and 2 Chronicles

The prophets can certainly be read on their own. Their messages frequently transcend the historical events of their day, especially scriptural passages or allusions that are found throughout the New Testament.

■ The Four Major Prophets

Isaiah lived in Jerusalem during the eighth century B.C. He may have been a priest, but that is not certain. He was married and had two sons. His period of most prophetical activity was from 742 to 687 B.C. The book of Isaiah consists of sixty-six chapters in which you find laments and warnings about Jerusalem and prophecies and proclamations against foreign nations that threaten the Jewish people.

Jeremiah was born around 650 B.C. He was a priest and an active prophet from 627 to 580 B.C. His prophesies frequently got him into trouble. Once, some people conspired to kill him, another time he was put in jail, and another time he was tried for blasphemy. The book of Jeremiah has fifty-one chapters. The book of Lamentations follows the book of Jeremiah. It consists of five poems. For a long time, it was attributed to Jeremiah, but many modern scholars disagree.

Associated with Jeremiah is Baruch. Baruch was a friend of Jeremiah and he wrote down a large number of Jeremiah's discourses. Baruch was not considered a prophet.

Ezekiel was a priest and was married. Ezekiel and his wife were deported to Babylon by Nebuchadnezzar in 597 B.C. Ezekiel was active as a prophet for thirty years from 593 to 563 B.C. His book has forty-eight chapters divided into four parts: (1) threatening discourses before the fall or Jerusalem, (2) prophesies against other nations, (3) discourses of promise after the fall of Jerusalem, and (4) prophesies about the restoration of Jerusalem and the temple.

Ezekiel is popular for his visions. The following is the first part of the vision of the chariot of Yahweh.

> "I looked; a stormy wind blew from the North, a great cloud with flashing fire and brilliant light round it, and in the middle, in the heart of the fire, a brilliance like that of amber, and in the middle of what seemed to be four living creatures. They looked like this: they were of human form. Each had four faces, each had four wings. Their legs were straight; they had hooves like calves glittering like polished brass. Below their wings, they had human hands on all four sides corresponding to their four faces and four wings."

The prophet Daniel is not easy to identify. Some claim Daniel was a pious Jewish exile in Babylon, but modern day biblical scholars tend to doubt his credentials. Aside from the actual identity of the author, the book of Daniel is also very different from the other three prophets. There are no long discourses or oracles. He doesn't preach. The book of Daniel, with twelve chapters, is the shortest book of the four major prophets. Six stories and four dream visions comprise the book. The best known episode is Daniel in the lions' den.

Bible Appreciation Quiz for Chapter IV - the Prophets

Can you match prophet and prophecy?

Open your Bible and see if you can find who wrote these well-known prophetic passages. The answers can be found in Appendix A.

(1.) "There shall come forth a shoot from the stump of Jesse, a branch will grow from the root, and the spirit of the Lord shall rest upon him, the spirit of wisdom and understanding…."

_____

(2.) "They shall beat their swords into ploughshares, and their spears into pruning hooks; nation shall not lift up sword against nation, neither shall they learn war any more."

_____

(3.) "You, Bethlehem of Ephrata, you are the littlest of the clans of Judah. Out of you will come forth the ruler of Israel and his going forth shall be from eternity."

_____

(4.) "A time is coming, says the Lord, when I will make a new covenant with the house of Israel and the house of Judah. It will not be like the old covenant I made with their forefathers…."

_____

(5.) "The spirit of the Lord is upon me. He has sent me to proclaim the good news to the poor, to set captives free...."

_____

(6.) "Behold, a virgin shall conceive and bear a son, and his name shall be called Emmanuel."

_____

(7.) Who interpreted for King Belshazzar the message *"mene, mene, teqel, parqin"* that a hand wrote on the wall?

_____

■ The Wisdom Books of the Old Testament

The **Wisdom Books** of the Old Testament are writings about thoughts, philosophy, wisdom, ponderings, or religious expressions that do not fit into the category of historical or prophetical writings. Most of these books were written between 600 and 300 B.C.

The wisdom books of the Bible, also referred to as the "Writings," can be read in their entirety or in part at any time; their primary purpose and value is for inspiration, reflection, advice, and prayer. The books in this group are: Job, Psalms, Proverbs, Ecclesiastes, Song of Songs, Wisdom, Sirach, Esther, Tobit, and Judith.

In some way, the themes of these books are always concerned with wisdom. In many cases the wisdom is mere human experience having little to do with the basic theme of the Bible of God's dealings with man. Much of Israel's wisdom was influenced by their gentile contemporaries. These books differ greatly from the Historical and Prophetical books of the Old Testament.

Find where the following books are located in the Bible. The list of chapters with each of the books is for future reference, unless you want to take a look at them now.

Job	This book is about the discussion of the meaning of suffering carried on by Job and some of his friends (Eliphaz, Bildad, Zophar, and Elihu). The basic lesson in this book is: Faith must remain even when understanding fails. *See especially Chapters: 1, 2, 3, 38, and 40.*

Proverbs	This is a collection of wise sayings. Most of this book is not particularly religious in content. One of the most well-known statements in Proverbs is "The fear of the Lord is the beginning of wisdom." [Pr 1:7 and 9:10] *See especially chapters 1, 26, 27.*
Ecclesiastes	This is seemingly a pessimistic view of the plight of mankind. The most well-known statement in Ecclesiastes is: "Vanity of vanities, all is vanity. What does a man gain by all the toil at which he toils under the sun?" [Ecc 1: 2] *See especially chapters 1, 3, 9, 12.*
Wisdom (Wisdom of Solomon)	Notice that wisdom is seen as a female spirit. "Wisdom begins with the sincere desire for instruction, care for instruction means loving her, loving her means keeping her love, attention to her laws guaranteed incorruptibility, and incorruptibility brings us near to God…" [Ws 6:17-19] *See especially chapters 1 and 2*

Sirach
(Ecclesiasticus)

Collection of sayings on practical wisdom by Jesus, son of Sirach. As in the book of Wisdom, wisdom is seen as a female spirit. "The crown of wisdom is the fear of the Lord: she makes peace and health flourishes." [Si 1:17-19]
See especially chapter 1.

Psalms

A collection of 150 poems and hymns written at different times during the history of the Israelites. Psalms come in different forms. There are royal Psalms which are directed to the king, which could be anything from the, enthronement of the king, prayers for the king, and a battle prayer for victory. A number of the Psalms are hymns which are usually of praise or thanksgiving. There are lamentations and supplications, both for an individual or for the community. Some Psalms are prophetic; some are historical meditations. The most famous Psalm is the Good Shepherd, Psalm 23.

Song of Songs
(Canticle of Canticles)

A series of love songs in which the lover and loved are united, then apart, lost and then found. "I am black, but beautiful..." [Sg 1:5]; "Love is strong as death..." [Sg 8:6]

Bible Appreciation Quiz for Chapter IV

See if you can find…

Write your answers on the line below the question.

With the various outlines of the books of the Old Testament you have already reviewed, take a moment to see if you can find some of the following well-known episodes or verses. Find the story or episode in the Bible and indicate chapter/verse reference in the blank space. If you don't want to interrupt your reading, then continue the narrative that follows this quiz and come back later to this quiz. You can also check Appendix A at the end of the book.

(1.) Where do you find the story of the Tower of Babel?

_____

(2.) When Daniel was thrown into the lion's den?

_____

(3.) When seven brothers offered themselves in martyrdom?

_____

(4.) When did Jacob get Esau's birth right?

_____

(5.) Who cut off Samson's long hair?

_____

(6.) When did the walls of Jericho collapse?

_____

(7.) When did Moses receive the Ten Commandments?

_____

(8.) Where do you find the story of Jezebel and all her wicked deeds?

_____

(9.) When did Elijah walk 40 days?

_____

(10.) When was Jacob tricked by Laban to work seven extra years?

_____

(11.) Who was the last king of Judah blinded and taken into captivity?

_____

(12.) Where do you find the story of the great-grandmother of King David?

_____

(13.) When did the angel change Jacob's name to Israel?

_____

✝

Chapter V: Reading and Understanding the New Testament

■ Preliminary Considerations

Catholics, as a rule, are more familiar with the New Testament than with the Old Testament, and usually feel more comfortable with the New Testament than with the old. This is understandable because the person of Jesus is the focus of the New Testament. The Old Testament is not as easily defined in terms of a person. The worship that Catholics experience in the annual liturgical calendar carries one through the life and teachings of Jesus. At Sunday Mass, there are two New Testament readings and only one Old Testament reading. The implied message here is that the New Testament is more important than the Old Testament. And, in fact, it is.

Even though this familiarity with the New Testament may be true, many Catholics have never read the entire New Testament. What they know is what they have heard at Mass or learned in religious education programs. And, even those who have read the entire New Testament may have finished it and still had many questions about it.

The following ideas about the New Testament as sacred scripture can help you achieve a greater appreciation of the New Testament when you read it. One of these preliminary ideas is how is the New Testament is divided or grouped into different kinds of books.

As a matter of convenience, and with some contrived similarity with the Old Testament, Bible study has made the New Testament fit a mold similar to that found in the Old Testament. One particular mold is to group the New Testament Books into the same categories as the Old Testament books. Although Catholic Bible study today is getting away from this traditional approach to some extent, it is still commonly used. For the Old Testament, the sacred books were grouped into three main categories:*

—Historical books

—Prophetical books

—Writings (or Sapiential Books)

* [Note: See "Understanding and Reading the Old Testament"]

Traditionally, these same three categories were applied to the New Testament books.

Historical books	Record of events during the life of Jesus on earth and the early Church. These books are the four Gospels—Matthew, Mark, Luke, and John, and Acts of the Apostles.
Prophetical Books	There is only one book placed in this category, the Apocalypse, or Revelation, attributed to John.

Epistles of Paul (14 in number)

Epistles of Peter (2)

Writings or Wisdom Books   Epistle of James (1)

Epistle of Jude (1)

Epistles of John (3)

This three-fold grouping is mentioned here because it was taught many years as an important aspect of understanding the Bible, and as a way of demonstrating how the New Testament reflects the Old Testament. Today, however, Catholic Bible study tends to avoid this grouping because the terms may be misunderstood as they apply to the Bible. For example, writing that is historical in our minds today is considered to be fairly accurate account of who did what, when, where, and why. And designating some books of the Bible historical leads many readers to expect the same precision in the New Testament historical books. And, that is not necessarily the case with the four Gospels. Acts of the Apostles fits historical criteria a little better than the four Gospels.

■ Prophecy and Apocalypse

The same caveat applies to the use of "Prophetical" when describing the "Apocalypse." In contemporary parlance, prophesying is generally understood as predicting or foretelling what is going to happen in the future. If one does not understand what the apocalyptic style of writing is, then the Apocalypse of John can be seen as a frightening prophecy of things to come. But there is a clear distinction between the prophets of the Old Testament and the writers of apocalyptic stories. The Old Testament prophets received their message by "hearing the word of God." On the other hand, the author of an apocalyptic revelation received the message in a vision. If you are aware that the apocalyptic style of literature was a kind of coded message to encourage its readers during times of persecution and great difficulty, then Apocalypse comes across as a book of encouragement and optimism.

■ Wisdom Books

Finally, classifying the epistles of the New Testament in the same category of literature as the "Wisdom" of the Old Testament is to really stretch the meaning. There is little ground of comparison between the content and style of the New Testament Epistles and the Old Testament books such as Job, Psalms, Ecclesiastes, Song of Songs, Wisdom, Proverbs, and several others.

In reading and understanding the New Testament, it is more useful to know something about where the book was written and who the intended audience was. For example, what was the reason for apostle Paul writing a letter to the Romans? Or, was Paul the author of the letter to the Hebrews, or did someone else write it? Were the three epistles of John written by John the apostle, or another John? Delving at length into these questions is not in the scope of this introduction to the Bible, but they are great areas to investigate for a more profound understanding of the Bible and its value in our spiritual search and journey toward God.

■ New Testament Historical Books

The four Gospels are far and above the most important books of the New Testament and for readers of the Gospels, the most important books of the entire Bible. The Gospels provide all we know about Jesus

Christ, his life and works, his passion and death, and his resurrection and return to the Father.

The importance of the four Gospels was clearly demonstrated in the early Christian community. "Among the sacred Scriptures available to the early Christians, the four Gospels were the most frequently copied of all the parts of the sacred Scriptures."

[Alfred Wikenhauser, *New Testament Introduction*, 1958.
This is a classic study of the circumstances surrounding the origin
of each book of the New Testament, the formation of the Cano,
and the history of the transmission of the texts.]

The first three Gospels, Matthew, Mark, and Luke are designated the "synoptics" (roughly meaning seen together) because they have many similarities. They are not identical in either approach or intended audience.

■ Matthew

Matthew, one of the twelve apostles, composed his gospel sometime during 80–90 A.D., and wrote it for Jewish converts living in Palestine. His purpose was to prove that Jesus Christ was the messiah that was foretold in the Old Testament. Matthew began his gospel by establishing Jesus's family lineage. "This is the list of the ancestors of Jesus Christ, a descendant of David, who was a descendant of Abraham.

From Abraham to King David the following ancestors are listed: Abraham, Isaac, Jacob, Judah and his brothers; then Perez and Zerah (their mother was Tamar), Hezron, Ram, Amminadab, Nahshon, Salmon, Boaz (his mother was Rahab), Obed (his mother was Ruth), Jesse, and King David.

From David to the time when the people of Israel were taken into exile in Babylon the following ancestors are listed: David, Solomon (his mother was the woman who had been

Uriah's wife), Rehoboam, Abijah, Asa, Jehoshaphat, Jehoram
Uzziah, Jotham, Ahaz, Hezekiah, Manaseh, Amon, Josiah,
and Jehoiachin and his brothers.

From the time after the exile in Babylon to the birth of
Jesus, the following ancestors are listed: Jehoiachin, Shealtiel,
Zerubbabel, Abiud, Eliakim, Azor, Zadok, Achim, Eliud,
Eleazar, Matthan, Jacob, and Joseph, who married Mary, the
mother of Jesus, who was called the Messiah.

So then there were 14 generations from David Abraham
and 14 from David to the exile in Babylon and 14 from then
to the birth of the Messiah." In the Jewish mindset, one's
genealogy was the most important evidence of authenticity.

[Translation of *The New Catholic Study Bible*, 1985]

Perhaps the most famous part of Matthew's gospel is the Sermon
on the Mount, the eight beatitudes. The eight beatitudes are not found
in any of the other gospels.

■ Mark

Mark was not an apostle and knew nothing about Jesus until
years after the death of Jesus. Mark came to know about the life
and work of Jesus by being apostle Peter's translator. He probably
wrote his gospel in Rome some years after Peter was martyred in
65 A.D. Mark directed his gospel to gentile Christians. He sought
to strengthen the faith of his audience writing about the deeds of
Jesus. Mark was noticeably different from Matthew. His gospel
began with "This is the Good News about Jesus Christ, the Son of
God." It began as the prophet Isaiah had written:" Behold, I send
my messenger before thy face, who shall prepare thy way; the voice

of one crying in the wilderness: Prepare the way of the Lord, make his paths straight." Jesus's genealogy, so important to the Jewish Christians, was not even mentioned in Mark's gospel. Mark got started and jumped right into Jesus's mission.

[Translation of *The New Catholic Study Bible*, 1985]

■ Luke

Luke, like Mark, was not one of the twelve apostles. He learned about Jesus through his association with the apostles Barnabas and Paul. His gospel, the longest of the three synoptics, was geared toward gentile Christians. He wrote it around 75–85 A.D. In his work on the life and works of Jesus, he was more attuned to the chronological and historical aspect of Jesus. Although not an apostle, Luke had many sources about Jesus, not just what he learned from Barnabas and Paul. He began his gospel with "Dear Theophilus: Many people have done their best to write a report of the things that have taken place among us. They wrote what we have been told by those who saw these things from the beginning and who proclaimed the message. And so, Your Excellency, because I have carefully studied all these matters from their beginning, I thought it would be good to write an orderly account for you. I do this so that you will know the full truth about everything which you have been taught."

[Translation of *The New Oxford Annotated Bible,* 1977]

An interesting point in Luke's gospel, and not as famous as Matthew's, is Luke's version of the beatitudes. Instead of eight beatitudes, Luke listed four beatitudes and four "woes" or curses.

"But woe to you that are rich, for you have received your consolation. Woe to you that are full now, for you shall hunger. Woe to you who laugh now, for you shall mourn and weep. Woe to you, when all men speak well of you, for so their fathers did for the false prophets."

In the second century A.D., Tatian, an Assyrian Christian, wrote a book titled, *Gospel by Means of the Four.* He formatted the book in four columns comparing each of the Gospels episode by episode. (It could not be compared chapter by chapter or verse by verse because chapters and verses were not applied to the Scriptures for another thousand years.) Tatian's book is known by a Greek word *Diatessaron*, (roughly translated "through the four"). The first three columns easily demonstrated that Matthew, Mark, and Luke had many similarities as mentioned above. On the other hand, in John's column very little coincided with the other three.

■John

When you compare John with the synoptics, only a small part of synoptic material is found in John and much of that is not completely in agreement. So different it is, John's gospel is in a class by itself.

(1) Of the twenty-nine miracles reported in the synoptics, John only uses two: the multiplication of bread and walking on water. He reports miracles not mentioned in the synoptics.

(2) The four Gospels have discourses of Jesus, but John has none that are like the synoptic discourses.

(3) The synoptics mention only one Passover; John writes about three.

There are many more differences in John.

John was an apostle very close to Jesus. He did not begin his gospel with any earthly reference to Jesus, Son of God, or his words and works as Matthew, Mark, and Luke did. John started beyond earth; he started beyond time. "In the beginning was the Word, and the Word was with God, and the Word was God. He was in the beginning with God; all things were made through him, and without him not anything made was made. In him was life, and the life was the light of men. The light shines in the darkness, and the darkness has not overcome it."

[Translation of *The New Oxford Annotated Bible*, 1977]

■ Acts (or Acts of the Apostles)

Luke, the same person who wrote the gospel, wrote the Acts. He wrote it sometime around 70 A.D. The Acts is a story about the growth of Christianity and the spread of the gospel throughout the known world, ending up in Rome which was considered the center of the world.

The book begins with a brief introduction and an account of the Ascension of Jesus. The main portion of the book can be divided into three parts: (1) the Jewish Christian community, chapters 1–6; (2) the beginning of the Gentile mission and the introduction of Saul (Paul); (3) A brief period of Barnabas and Paul working together, then the work of Paul, the apostle to the Gentiles.

Bible Appreciation Quiz for Chapter V

The answers to these questions are in Appendix A

(1.) How many gospels are considered "synoptic?"

_____

(2.) Where do you go to find the eight beatitudes?

_____

(3.) Which gospel used a genealogy to demonstrate that Jesus was truly the Royal lineage?

_____

(4.) In what gospel do you find the miracle of the multiplication of the loaves of bread?

_____

(5.) Which gospel reports Jesus bringing a dead man back to life?

_____

(6.) Which evangelist wrote about the miracle of changing water into wine?

_____

(7.) Was Matthew the evangelist who wrote for an audience of gentile Christians?

_____

(8.) How many journeys of St. Paul are recorded in the Acts of the apostles?

_____

✝

Chapter VI: General Observations about the Bible

■ More on the "Book of Many Books": Groups of Books and Literary Forms

As you get a feeling for the overall content of the Bible, from Genesis to Apocalypse, and see that the Bible is a book of many books, it is good to point out that in the collection of the various books of the Bible, there are groups of writings. An older and more traditional method of grouping had three categories: historical, prophetical, and wisdom books. This threefold division was conveniently applied to both the Old Testament and the New Testament. In the Old Testament, historical books cover more or less a chronological history of the Hebrew people and their understanding as the Chosen People of God. The prophetical books are the writings of the prophets, the special spokesmen of God during Old Testament times. The final group of books, the wisdom books, is a small group of seven books loosely linked with philosophical ideas or views about the virtue of wisdom.

More recent groupings of the books of the Bible have four groups. In addition to the historical, prophetical, and wisdom books, is the Pentateuch. The difference in the groupings is solely the special designation of the Pentateuch, which is a division based on the Hebrew "Torah." The Pentateuch consists of the first five books of the Bible: Genesis, Exodus, Leviticus, Numbers, and Deuteronomy. In the Hebrew Bible, these five books, the Torah, were referred to as the "Law." Catholic biblical scholarship in the last decades of the twentieth century began adopting this four-fold division as a more accurate reflection of the Old Testament scriptures. Under this four-fold grouping, the list of the "historical books begin with the book of Joshua," rather than the traditional list which begins with the book of Genesis. The English language version of the famous "Jerusalem Bible" presents this latter kind of division.

[See the section on Understanding and Reading the Old Testament and the list how the books of the Bible are grouped, pp. 49-55]

Another aspect of the Bible as a book of many books is the variety of the kinds of books and the literary style in which they are presented. Referred to as the "literary forms" or "genre" of the Bible, the different ways of presenting ideas and message clearly illustrate the fact that the Bible was not just written from beginning to end by one writer. Literary types or genre in the Bible include: prose (historical narratives), poetry (Psalms), songs (Psalms), hymns, battle stories (Deborah, Judith), parables (Jesus), sermons (prophets), exhortations, statistical data (Leviticus, Numbers), doctrinal teaching (Leviticus), historical novels (Tobit, Judith, Esther), rituals (Leviticus), laws and regulations (Exodus, Deuteronomy), laments (Psalms, prophets), historical events and reporting (Kings and Chronicles), philosophical reflection (Job, Proverbs, Ecclesiastes, Wisdom), letters and epistles (Paul, Jude, James, Peter, John), genealogies (Genesis, Numbers), memoirs (Mark, Luke), oracles (prophets), and proverbs.

The Catholic Church does not teach or profess that the Bible was dictated by God. It does not teach that the Bible was written down by men in some kind of trance through which God transmitted his message to mankind. There is no official doctrine of the Catholic Church about how the Bible was written. The generally accepted position is that the Bible as we know it today was developed over a very prolonged process and from numerous sources and subject to many external influences. The teaching of the Catholic Church is that the Bible is the inspired word of God. Just how the inspiration took place in the process of getting the Divine message written down is not clearly explained. But it is a doctrine of Catholic faith that the Bible is the inspired word of God. The role of the Holy Spirit in producing the Bible, as well as in interpreting the Bible, is also a doctrine of Catholic faith. The Catholic Church does not claim to know or try to explain everything about the Bible. The Catholic Church does proclaim that the Holy Spirit is the true author of the Bible, and through the Spirit's inspiration, humans, with their talents, limitations, faults, emotions, perceptions, skills, and insights, were involved in the process of writing down the divine message.

A brief example of this can be found in the Pentateuch. Traditionally, Moses was credited with being the author of the Pentateuch. These first five books of the Bible cover a historical period from the creation of the world to the death of Moses. We do not have a fixed date for the death of Moses, but the general timeframe is 1300–1250 B.C. Biblical research during the last 100 years, based on the study of ancient languages, literature, and cultures, plus history, has concluded that the final rendition of the Pentateuch, as we have it today was accomplished somewhere between 700 B.C. and 500 B.C.

The existence of literary forms in the Bible is a major aspect of the Catholic understanding and interpretation of the Bible. Just as the

Catholic Church does not teach that the Bible was written by persons in some kind of trance or special vision, neither does the Catholic Church teach a literal, word for word understanding of the Bible. The Catholic Church's and mainstream Protestant denominations' interpretations of the Bible differ from the Fundamentalists' interpretation of the Bible. Fundamentalism generally teaches that the Bible is inspired "and the inspiration extends not just to the message God wished to convey, but to the very words chosen by the sacred writers."

[Source: art, "Fundamentalism," Catholic Answers; http://www.catholic.com/Library/fundamentalism.asp]

■Getting still more familiar with the Bible: the Parade

At this point, we'll take a lengthier look at the entire Bible and expand on what we have already seen. We examine the course of the Bible story, where it begins, which periods it passes through, and where it is going. We will find stories of the famous people and determine what message God is revealing.

Imagine yourself on some high vantage point where you can view what is going on far below. Maybe it is a mountain lookout where you can observe a long migration of animals passing in an endless trek from one place to another. Maybe it is a tall building where you can look down and see the entire Macy's parade from beginning to end. That is the kind of position we take at this point: we want to see the whole procession or parade of the Bible. From our high vantage point we can see the beginning, the end, and everything in between.

From our incredible observation post we look down on the parade of God's revelation to humankind. We can see the beginning of creation and the well-known stories of Adam and Eve, Cain and Able, Noah and the ark, and the Tower of Babel. The parade continues on. There is Abraham and a key moment in this history when a man totally and unreservedly puts his faith and trust in God. Then come the patriarchs: Isaac, Jacob (whose name was changed to Israel because he struggled with God), and Joseph, who was sold in slavery by his brothers. [Book of **Genesis.**]

Then, we move to the life of Moses, seeing the events that led to the delivery of the Israelites from slavery in Egypt. Next are the scenes in the desert and wilderness, leading to another key moment in the story of God's revelation: the encounter of Moses with God on Mount Sinai and the Ten Commandments. This is the moment of the first covenant of God with mankind. Moses, the great leader out of slavery becomes the great law giver. We watch Israelites struggle with God because of faintheartedness, lack of trust in Yahweh, and idolatry of false gods. [Books of **Exodus, Leviticus, Numbers, Deuteronomy**]

The Promised Land is reached, and Joshua leads the Israelites to victory. They settle in the Promised Land, with the land divided among twelve tribes [Book of **Joshua**]. We watch the Israelites in the Promised Land as they are governed by a number of leaders referred to as "Judges."[Book of **Judges**] After this, we can see the prophet Samuel and the role he plays in establishing the kingdom of the Israelites [**I** and **II Samuel**]. The great King David is followed by his son King Solomon. Family disputes and tribal animosity result in the division of the kingdom into the north and south, the Kingdom of Israel and the Kingdom of Judah. If we watch time closely, we see it is a gradual but complete failure as idolatry, child sacrifice, and immorality result in the disintegration of the bonds between Yahweh and his chosen people. The Northern Kingdom is crushed by the powerful Assyrian Empire and its people are scattered. The Kingdom of Judah collapses about 130 years later. Those who survive the horrors of war are taken away in exile to Babylon. The pride of Judah, the city of Jerusalem, with its great defensive wall, the majestic temple, the palaces, buildings, and homes, is utterly destroyed. Those left from the Israelite nation in exile have decades to remember the shattered covenant with God and the failure of their way of life. They remember and weep [**1 and 2 Kings**, and **1** and **2 Chronicles**].

Great prophets live in these times but their words fall mostly on deaf ears. [Books of the major prophets: **Isaiah, Jeremiah, Ezekiel, and Daniel** as well as the twelve minor prophets: **Hosea, Joel, Amos, Obadiah, Jonah, Micah, Nahum, Habakkuk, Zephaniah, Haggai, Zechariah, and Malachi.**]

Again, from our vantage point, we see a later period when the exiles from Israel are allowed to return to their home land and they struggle to rebuild Jerusalem and the temple [Books of **Ezra** and **Nehemiah**]. The people manage to rebuild the nation, but nothing they do matches the glory of the kingships of David and Solomon. Politically, the land of Israel is beleaguered constantly by the stronger nations and empires.

Here the parade of Salvation History has noticeable gaps and we look hard to find some continuity. For Israel and Judaism, God's revelations cease. God's presence among his chosen people can no longer be found. We notice only a few slight movements in the 300-year gap of this great parade. With some exceptions, the people here are moving along the parade of life aimlessly, confused, in mental blindness, and spiritual darkness. While watching this great parade, we direct a telescope and get a closer image of some of the other details in this parade. We can look at the story of Ruth, the great grandmother of David [Book of **Ruth**]. We go to other periods and see the story of Tobit and his son, the daring exploits of Judith, and Esther, the Jewish maiden who became the queen of a Persian Emperor [Books of **Tobit**, **Judith**, and **Esther**]. We can focus our telescope on the time about two centuries before the birth of Jesus and see the exploits of the courageous Hebrew family of the Maccabees [**1 and 2 Maccabees**].

Then, as we search the next part of this great parade of God dealing with man, a star hovers over the parade, brightness grows, and Divine Light envelopes the world as the Son of God becomes the Son of Man. We observe the life of this Son of Man, we hear his words, we see his works, and we follow the events of his life and death. Only for a moment we are saddened, because after three days, the Son of God rises from the tomb [The four Gospels: **Matthew, Mark, Luke, John**]. He strengthens his apostles and directs them to carry the message to the ends of the world. With a sense of relief, we see that God, who we now call Father, has entered into a completely new and more powerful revelation and communication with humankind [**Acts of the Apostles**].

A new covenant is established. This covenant is forever. This is the Catholic understanding of what the church should be. Through the letters of Paul, Peter, Jude, James, and John, we read about the development of the church's reflection on itself, its mission, and the way the people should carry out their lives in community consciousness. [The epistles of **Paul** to the **Romans, Corinthians, Galatians, Ephesians, Philippians, Colossians, Thessalonians, Timothy, Titus,** and, **Philemon**; the epistle to the **Hebrews**; the epistles of **James, Peter, John,** and **Jude**]

As we scan the horizon looking at this parade, it seems to go beyond our sight. We cannot see exactly where it ends. But, we have been given the assurance that the Spirit of God is with us all the way, assuring us that all will be well no matter how difficult or even horrendous it might appear [**Apocalypse or Revelation**].

And, this parade we've seen from our high vantage point is a picture of the Bible from beginning to end, Genesis to Apocalypse.

■A brief comparison of the Catholic Bible and Protestant Bible

About every Catholic is aware that there is a Catholic Bible and a Protestant Bible, but not everyone knows what the difference is, or why. Earlier, we saw the difference is in the number of books in the Bible. The Protestant Bible has 66 books and the Catholic Bible has 72. The Protestant Bible has thirty-nine books in the Old Testament; the Catholic Bible has 45. There is no difference in the New Testament, which has twenty-seven books in both bibles. The reason for the difference lies in the Old Testament. There is a difference in the Hebrew language version of the Jewish Scriptures and the later Greek version of the Jewish Scriptures.

Why was there a Greek version of the Hebrew Scriptures? You can find the reason in the history of the Jewish people. The kingdom of the Hebrew people, which was at its height during the reigns of King David and King Solomon, began to deteriorate after the death of Solomon. The kingdom was divided in two. The Northern Kingdom was known as the Kingdom of Israel and the southern kingdom was known as the Kingdom of Judah. In 712 B.C., the Assyrians overran the Kingdom of Israel. The people of the Kingdom of Israel were scattered in many parts of the territories the Assyrians conquered. The Kingdom of Judah survived precariously for another 125 years and then fell under the onslaught of King Nebuchadnezzar of the Babylonian Empire in 587 B.C. Jerusalem was totally destroyed. At this time, most of the people of the southern kingdom who survived the war were taken into slavery and brought to Babylon. This was known as the great Babylonian Exile. So, basically, at this time, the traditional land of the Hebrew people, the land promised to Abraham, the land of the Patriarchs, the land where they had lived and flourished for 800 years was devastated. The Babylonian Exile came to an end in 537 B.C., when the Emperor

Cyrus of the Persians conquered Babylonia and sent the Jewish exiles back to their homeland. Not long after this (apparently as early as 500 B.C.), there were numerous communities in Egypt. As time went on, Jewish communities expanded to Syria, Asia Minor, Persia, Greece, and Italy. This displacement of Jewish people is commonly known as the Diaspora.

After several hundred years living in a world dominated by Hellenic culture and the Greek language, the Jewish people who lived outside of their homeland knew little of the Hebrew language. Over a period of 150–200 years, the Hebrew Scriptures were translated into Greek. In the second century B.C., in the great Egyptian city of Alexandria, a group of Greek-speaking Jews completed a translation of the Hebrew Scriptures. This translation was known as the Septuagint. It was widely accepted and used for generations as a faithful translation of the Hebrew Scriptures. The Septuagint, however, included holy books of the Jews that were written after the Babylonian Exile and more precisely after the period of Ezra and Nehemiah around 450 B.C., when the returnees from exile were rebuilding Jerusalem. These books were Maccabees 1 and 2, Tobit, Judith, Sirach, Wisdom, Baruch, and some parts of Daniel and Esther. The Jews of Jerusalem did not recognize these books as part of the collection of their holy writings. However, outside of Jerusalem, the Greek-speaking Jews did. The Greek translation had been in circulation for over 200 years by the time of Jesus. Hebrew was basically a dead language by this time. The Jews who lived outside ancient Palestine accepted the additional books in the Greek translation. The everyday language of the Jewish people was Aramaic, not Hebrew. The early Christian Church accepted the Greek version, and later along with this, the Latin translation of the Bible from the Septuagint by St. Jerome. The Catholic Church has long held that these books are truly part of the inspired books of the Bible. The Christian rejection of the seven books of the Septuagint did not happen in any significant way until the Protestant Reformation. The validity of the Septuagint Old Testament has been a disputed issue for the last 450 years. [Review the list of books in the section "Catholic Bibles and Protestant Bibles" pp.39-40]

This historical explanation answers the question "Why the Catholic Bible is different from the Protestant Bible?" But other questions remain.

Which Bible is the true Bible?

If the Catholic Church believes in the Bible, why doesn't it use the Bible and emphasize the Bible like the Protestant churches?

If the Bible is the inspired Word of God, why don't Catholics believe every word in it?

The study of Bible appreciation should provide satisfactory answers to these important questions. The answers rest in the Catholic Church's understanding of **what** Divine revelation is, and **how** God reveals things to mankind.

Bible Appreciation Quiz for Chapter VI

Answers to these questions are in Appendix A.

(1.) Does the Catholic Church teach that the Bible was dictated by God?

_____

(2.) Does the Catholic Church teach that the Bible is the inspired word of God?

_____

(3.) Why was there a Greek translation of the Hebrew Bible?

_____

(4.) What is meant by the Canon of the New Testament?

_____

(5.) What was the name given to the Greek translation of the Hebrew Bible?

_____

(6.) Does the Catholic Church teach that the human writers of the Bible were in a trance?

_____

(7.) What do you understand about the meaning of the parade?

_____

_____

Chapter VII: The Essence of Bible Appreciation

■ What is the Bible in 25 words or less?

When I taught each new session of Bible appreciation, someone invariably asked the question "Can you define what the Bible is in more than seven words, but less than twenty-five?" That may not have been exactly the way the query was worded, but it was what the question meant. In other words, the person wanted an answer to "What is the Bible?" described more fully than the standard seven-word answer, "The Bible is the Word of God." But the questioner wanted an answer that was not so complete and thorough that it would take an hour to explain. So my answer in twenty-five words or less was: **The Bible is a written record of God's efforts to communicate with man and man's response to God. It is a love story.**

Understood in that way, the Bible is relevant today, it was relevant yesterday, and it will be relevant tomorrow.

Take a closer look at this answer. The Bible is a *written record* of God's efforts to communicate with man. God communicates with man in many ways through: the awe and magnificence of creation; our reasoning processes; prayer and meditation; and the experience of love, goodness, truth, and beauty. The Holy Spirit is involved in all these ways. The Church is another way God communicates with man. [Notice the choice of verb tense, "communicates," not "communicated" in past times. Through the written record in the Bible, God still communicates with man.]

This answer to the question deliberately avoids using "The Word of God." The main reason is that the phrase "The Word of God" implies infallibility, immutability, completeness, total truth, and inerrancy. As a complete definition of the Bible, the statement "The Bible is the Word of God," is both inadequate and misleading. For Catholics, this answer simply is not good enough, because the Bible is the Word of God written in the words of men. The Catholic Church teaches that the authors of the sacred Scriptures wrote God's message under the guidance and inspiration of the Holy Spirit, but they were limited by their own language, culture, environment, and historical times.

Once again we use the statement "the Word of God in the words of men." There is a human element in the Bible, which is neither infallible nor error-free. Our understanding and interpretation of the Bible must take into account as much as possible the many human elements in the sacred texts. Catholics do not accept all the words of the Bible as literal truth and as absolute reality. Example: the story of Creation says God created the world and all its creatures in six days. Literally, we take that to mean that in six 24-hour days (as the book of Genesis expressed in the image of morning and evening) God created the world. Religious Creationism professes that as the exact historical and scientific truth. The Catholic Church, as well as many Christians, does not believe the world was created in six 24-hour days. Now, the phrase "The Word of God" properly understood is all these things: eternal, immutable, infallible, and absolute truth. Unquestionably. But the Word of God, as is so magnificently expressed in the prologue to John's gospel, is the Second Person in the Divine Being. Jesus Christ is the incarnate expression of that Divine Word. Jesus is the fullness of God's Word. [see Jn1:1–14]

When we affirm that the Bible is the absolute Word of God we make ourselves vulnerable to all kinds of traps and fallacies. If we profess the Bible is The Word of God (and that the word is eternal, unchanging, free from any and all kinds of error, and unchallengeable), then the book we hold in our hands must be the holiest thing a human can touch. As such, no matter what the Bible says, it has to be true. Whether the mind can understand it or not, it is true and one must accept to it. Whether or not it defies our senses and reasoning capability, we must submit our intelligence to it. In this mindset, what the Bible says is unquestionable truth. Believe it and be saved. Don't believe it and be damned.

Many Catholics do not ascribe to such a restricted belief. Why? Because it is impossible to follow. For one, which Bible edition is the true one? The English one? The French one? The German one? The Spanish one? If English, then which English version? The King James Version? The "Good News for Modern Man" version? The Jerusalem Bible version? To claim the Bible is The Word of God (with all its omnipotent attributes) means that not one word can be changed. Yet, there are dozens of different versions in the English language. Which version is sacrosanct? Moreover, the Bible has been translated into over a thousand languages and dialects. In answer to that, some people may say, "Well, yes, translations do introduce some unfortunate word changes to the original Bible. So, all the more reason for us to read the Bible in Hebrew and Greek." That does not solve any problems either. What is the original Hebrew manuscript of Old Testament writings? Where is this book kept? Also, which is the original Greek manuscript of the New Testament? Where is this book found? To continue in this search for the "real Bible" would be silly and fruitless. There is no "original Bible" in the sense of one neatly packaged volume. The Old

Testament part of the Bible is not a single book, and the New Testament is not a single book.

The Old Testament (which is actually a Christian term, not a Jewish term) is a collection of writings from many centuries that the Jewish religion put together and determined its contents. The New Testament is a collection of writings from many decades that the Christian church got together and determined its contents. The precise elements of the Bible, both the Old and the New Testaments, were decided by committee. The official list of the Scriptures is called the "Canon." The first approved collection of books is called the Jewish Canon. The second is called the Christian Canon and it includes the Old Testament and the New Testament. A holy writing that deserved to be on the approved list is referred to as a "canonical book." Although the Jewish scriptures were largely defined about 400 B.C., a definitive Jewish Canon did not occur until the Council of Jamnia in 90 A.D. The Christian Scriptures, although largely defined by about 150 A.D., were not declared to be part of the Christian Canon until the Council of Trent in the sixteenth century. Catholics do believe that the Holy Spirit guided this selection and approval process. The Bible we have today is rightly called the work of the Holy Spirit. Catholic belief is that the Bible is the inspired word of God. The Catholic Church does not have a simple, concise definition of "inspiration" when applied to the writing of the sacred Scriptures.

Whereas the Catholic Church reveres and proclaims The Word of God in all its liturgical prayers and sacraments, it does not claim that the Bible is "The" Word of God and must be believed literally in every thing it says and how it says it. This borders on absurdity because it would imply that man's expression of ideas in the Bible is also eternal, infallible, and immutable. Such a claim, however, has been used by some Christian preachers to instill fear and achieve submission of followers.

Let's continue our examination of the definition of the Bible "in 25 words or less." The Bible has been described as a great love story. For the person who takes it to mean exactly that, the Bible is a beautiful companion to life. And, that is what it is meant to be: A companion, not a torturer of the soul and spirit. That is why my answer is always "The Bible is a written record of God's efforts to communicate with man and man's response to God. It is a love story."

Such a description covers God's message of love in—

...the origins of man and all creation;

...man's original (innate) conflict with God;

...God's steadfast love in his promises to Adam and Eve and Cain, to Abraham, Isaac, Israel (Jacob), Joseph;

...God's Covenant with the Hebrew people through Moses, Joshua, Judges, Kings, the exile, and return from exile;

...the foundation and preparation work for the coming Messiah;

...the incarnate Word and the visible events affecting the message of salvation; and

...the formation and growth of the Mystical Body.

This description records man's response to God's communication in—

...creation and the original fall from grace;

...sin in all of mankind;

...Abraham's faith and humanity;

...Patriarchs, their faith and weaknesses;

...fidelity and infidelity;

...the Exodus and the enthusiasm;

...the Wilderness and the peoples' griping;

...the covenant of Sinai and forsaking that covenant;

...Joshua and the Promised Land;

...Judges and backsliding;

...Saul and failure;

...David and weaknesses;

...Solomon and his detour;

...the divided Kingdom;

...the exile and conversion;

...the return from exile, lack of interest, laxity and a watered-down covenant; and

...the coming of Jesus and the Church with its ups and downs just like the people of the Old Testament.

The Bible is a mirror in which we can see ourselves as individuals and as community, as God asks us to be, and as we really are. The Bible is a treasure that we can draw from all our lives. And, throughout the Bible, from beginning to end, the message is that God is in charge no matter how horrible it might seem to us. We learn Jesus is Lord, and the Holy Spirit is Life.

■A Holistic Approach to the Bible

Now that we've seen the basic composition of the Bible, how it is divided into the Old Testament and the New Testament, what books make up the Bible, why there might be differences between traditional Catholic bibles and traditional Protestant bibles, the official statement of the Catholic Church about the Bible in the Vatican Council's Dogmatic Constitution on Divine Revelation, we can at last come to a possible approach for Catholics of the twenty-first century. This approach that can bring Catholics to accept the Bible and understand it as a book relevant to their faith and daily lives, or, as we put it at the start, to learn the Bible, love the Bible, and live the Bible.

A holistic approach sees the Bible as an integral unit which is not something we Catholics, and non-Catholic Christians, have successfully accomplished until now.

■What exactly is this holistic approach to the Bible?

Let's look at the Bible again. Take your Bible in your hands. Let it be your favorite: a family Bible that has been passed down through several generations; a favorite version, translation, or language edition of the Bible; the Bible that was given to you when you made your confirmation; the pretty hand Bible in the white leather binding with the gilded edges that your Aunt Emma gave you. Or even, and this might be a rarity among Catholics, the Bible with a broken binding and pages stained and worn from having been turned so many times from constant reading.

It is a complete Bible in one volume. The first book is Genesis. The last book is Apocalypse, or Revelation. Now, it doesn't really matter if you have a traditional Catholic Bible, or a traditional Protestant Bible. The Catholic Bible will be a little thicker because it has more to it than the Protestant Bible. That doesn't matter much in the holistic approach to understanding the Bible.

The holistic approach to the Bible looks at the entire cluster of books (whether sixty-six or seventy-two) as one single, solitary book. What does that mean, as a single, solitary book? Isn't that what the Bible is? Yes, it is but we tend to break up the Bible in several ways. We can talk about the Old Testament and the New Testament. We can talk about the historical books, the prophetical books, and the wisdom books. Or, we can talk about every individual book. We have sometimes described the Bible as a small library. We may have looked at the Bible as the "History of Salvation."

The holistic approach looks at the Bible from beginning to end as one creation, one great work of Divine Revelation, written over a period of 2,000 years in human time, but just a moment in Holy Spirit time. This great divinely inspired work starts with something outside of time and outside of history, and ends the same way with something outside of time and outside of history. In between these two timeless, non-historical "some things" is a record of events, personalities, and thoughts that do take place in time, and have an historical nature about them. The two timeless, non-historical parts of the Bible are in the book of Genesis and the book of Revelation.

The first timeless part of the Bible happens "In the beginning..." The Bible starts in the "Beginning." The beginning of what? Of time? Of Creation? Of the Sun and Stars? Of water and land? Of animals?

Of man? The answer is yes and no to each of these questions. The best answer is that it is the beginning of the omniscient and omnipotent Eternal God's revelation of his nature.

The first distinct part of the Bible is not the book of Genesis. It is the first eleven chapters of Genesis. For the Catholic Church and for a significant number of Protestant denominations, the first eleven chapters of Genesis have, for quite some time, been understood as "pre-history." History, as is customarily accepted, is a definable point in time and space. Pre-history does not meet the criteria of time and space. Pre-history, as the term implies, is beyond the confines of time and space. That does not mean that it is not real, or that it did not happen, or that there is no factual basis. It simply means in our way of thinking, the events or actions written about in a pre-history, cannot be equated with our generally understood "historical event."

> [Note: There is serious disagreement between those Christians who believe the Bible is literally true in every word, and Christians who recognize the possibility of human error in the written expression of God's revelation. (Refer back to a brief discussion about Bible fundamentalism and why the Catholic Church does not accept this kind of understanding of the Bible, pp. 83-84)]

The second timeless, non-historical part of the Bible is the book of Revelation, also known as the Apocalypse. It is commonly taken to refer to the end of the world. The term "apocalypse" has evolved from its original meaning of a coded message in time of persecution to now portray a cataclysmic disaster. Some preachers like to wax eloquence on the imagery and their understanding of the message in the book of Revelation: angels and beasts, and epic struggles, the elect, and the damned. This kind of preaching has been going on for nearly 1,900 years. In its most distasteful form, apocalyptic preaching attempts to convert by fear. The end is near, repent. (As if we don't really need to repent if the end is not near?) For people who are ignorant of history, this kind of preaching works for a short time. The Catholic Church no longer engages in this kind of preaching, not because it shies away from fear and damnation, but because it teaches a more optimistic view of the coming of the Son of God and the establishment of his kingdom.

A holistic approach to the Bible, then, proceeds in this manner. The Bible is one complete written book. It begins with a prologue, progresses through a series of historical events, and ends with an epilogue.

■ Prologue and Epilogue

Our prologue is the first eleven chapters of Genesis, referred to as "pre-history." The epilogue is the book of Revelation. These two portions of the written word of God are not concerned with time or space. What are these two non-historical parts of the Bible concerned with? They are concerned with the presentation of universal and immutable divine truths.

What are these universal and immutable divine truths? These are the things that every person must know, what every person should be taught.

(1) God exists.

(2) God is the creator; his Divine Word is the source of everything. God is in charge.

(3) Everything God creates is good.

(4) Humankind is created by God and subject to him.

(5) God tells man and woman what to do, but they rebel against God's will.

(6) Rebellion against the will of God brings great suffering,

sorrow, deprivation, and pain

(7) Despite the rebellion, God desires union with mankind, and promises to set things right again.

In the prologue of the Bible, these truths are presented in several different stories, Adam and Eve, Cain and Abel, Noah and the flood, the Tower of Babel.

In the epilogue of the Bible, the book of Revelation, these divine truths are confirmed in their eternal reality.

(1) God exists, in ineffable majesty, splendor, and power.

(2) God is still in charge, but he has handed over control to the Son

(3) Away from God, Evil runs rampant.

(4) Those that are faithful to the will of God will be rewarded

(5) What might happen, the Son of God will triumph.

(6) Peace and happiness comes to those whose will conform to the Divine Will.

The book of Revelation ends with a prayer, "Come, Lord Jesus."

There is no time and space in the prologue or the epilogue of the Bible. The message in both transcends time and space. The basic divine teachings are valid always and everywhere.

Now that we understand the prologue and the epilogue of the Bible, what do we do with the large middle part?

That massive section from the story of Abraham beginning in chapter 12 of Genesis, all the way through the Old and New Testament to the last epistle, that of St. Jude. This major portion of the Bible, in a general sense, is historical in that it presents God's communication with humankind through events, times and places. We see the continuity of a kind of History of Salvation, beginning with Abraham and the Patriarchs, the time of Moses, Joshua and the Judges, the kings, the exile and the return from exile, Jewish life up to the birth of Jesus, his life and death, the beginning of the church. And through that history of some 1,800 years, we also read from the prophets, and other writers, whose messages reflect the times in which they wrote.

What does the holistic approach tell us about all this? See it in its entirety. The message is one of God trying to communicate with man and man's efforts at putting into practice what they believe to be God's communications and how it should be interpreted. We can see that the message in 1,800 years of God struggling with man is seminally contained in the message of the prologue, and confirmed in the epilogue. God creates all things. He communicates with humankind. Humankind struggles against the Divine Will. That might be viewed a bit simplistic. But is it?

In our time, as written in the Bible, God created. In God's time, God creates. He does so constantly, also in our time. This is where things can get complicated. One of the divine attributes is eternal. I think all Christians believe this. God is eternal. Eternity is endless. It is endless in two directions, forward and backward. There is no before and after. Another divine attribute is immutability. It cannot change or be changed. God does not change. The universe, as many scientists tell us today, is constantly expanding. Is it expanding by itself? No. God must be helping. On a macrocosmic scale, God must be busy creating more and more space so the expanding universe will have a place to go. God also continuously creates in a microcosmic scale, in us—each one of us, every nanosecond of our lives. God sustains us constantly. Our most important task in life is to find this abiding presence of God in our personal being as well as in coming to know and accept His will and submit our will to the Divine Will. We pray for this quite often and do it so fast we hardly know for what we have prayed: "Thy will be done on earth as it is in heaven."

This is what the middle part of the Bible, that large body between the prologue and the epilogue, tries to teach us. It is what Jesus taught. It is what the Church is supposed to teach.

Bible Appreciation Quiz for Chapter VII

Answers to these questions are in Appendix A

(1.) What is meant by "the word of God in the words of men?"

_____

_____

(2.) Where do they keep the original manuscript of the Old Testament?

_____

_____

(3.) What is the holistic approach to the Bible?

_____

_____

(4.) What is meant by "pre-history" in the Bible?

_____

_____

(5.) What are two divine attributes of God?

_____

_____

(6.) What is the difference between Apocalypse and Apocrypha?

_____

_____

(7.) When did the Catholic Church officially define the Christian Canon of the Bible?

_____

_____

✝

Chapter VIII: Catholic Church Teachings about the Bible

The Catholic Church has tried to maintain the integrity of the sacred Scriptures since the beginning of the Christian era. The Fathers of the Church in the second and third centuries wrote and preached about which of the many books being circulated were the authentic books of the sacred Scriptures. Following the patristic era, theologians and Christian writers wrote profusely on the use and authenticity of the books of the Bible and denounced errors of the flood of apocryphal books that were written at this time. Throughout the centuries, different church councils, both regional and ecumenical, have continued the guardianship of the sacred Scriptures.

The most definitive counsel on doctrine and issues regarding the Bible was the Council of Trent, as discussed earlier. After the Council of Trent, no significant teaching on the Bible occurred until 300 years later. The First Vatican Council (Vatican I) of 1869–70 affirmed the doctrine of the Council of Trent. Since the time of Vatican I, numerous popes have prepared encyclicals and papal statements regarding the Bible. Pope Leo XIII wrote the encyclical, *Providentissimus Deus*, in 1893. Pope Pius X issued a decree against modernism in 1907. Pope

Benedict XV promulgated the encyclical *Spiritus Paracletus* in 1926. Pope Pius XII issued the encyclical *Divino Afflante Spiritu* in 1949. And finally, the Second Vatican Council (Vatican II) in 1961–65 took a major step forward in reaffirming church doctrine on the Bible and at the same time addressing the value and importance of the pastoral application of the Bible and encouraging the laity to read the Bible.

■Dogmatic Constitution on Divine Revelation *(Dei Verbum)*

The Catholic Church's answers to the important questions asked in the previous section can be derived from the Church's Dogmatic Constitution on Divine Revelation. The *Dogmatic Constitution on Divine Revelation* is the Vatican II's pronouncement on the Bible. It was solemnly promulgated by Pope Paul VI in November 1965, and it is the basic concept of the Catholic Church about sacred Scripture. As such, it is a very important doctrinal document for all Catholics. It looks at the Bible in the context of the whole Christian doctrine of salvation. The following summary provides the main ideas of this document. Readers are encouraged to read the complete version.

A complete version of Dei Verbum can be found online at www.vatican.va/archive

■Preface:

"This present council wishes to set forth authentic teaching about Divine Revelation and about how it is handed on, so that by hearing the message of salvation, the whole world may believe; by believing, it may hope; and by hoping, it may love. "

■ Chapter I: Revelation Itself

God chose to reveal himself and make known to us the hidden purpose of his will. "Through this revelation, the invisible God, out of the abundance of his love, speaks to man as friends and lives among them, so that he may invite and take them into fellowship with Himself."

…. Creation is revelation witnessing to God.

…. God goes a step further and began manifesting himself

…. God sent his son to dwell among men and tell them the innermost realities of God.

…. The Christian dispensation is the definitive covenant that will not pass away.

■ Chapter II: The Transmission of Divine Revelation

God has seen fit to it that His revelation would last forever in full integrity and be handed on for all generations.

Apostolic transmission, or "*Traditio*" (Sacred Tradition), is to be preserved until the end of time.

…. Close connection between Scripture and Sacred Tradition.

… Scripture and Tradition are one sacred deposit of God's word.

■ Chapter III: Divine Inspiration and the Interpretation of Scripture

.... The Bible contains divinely revealed realities.

.... The Bible teaches without error the truth that God wanted to put into writing.

.... Because God speaks through human fashion, we must investigate the real meaning of the Scriptures.

.... Scripture must be read and interpreted according to the same Spirit by whom it was written.

■ Chapter IV: The Old Testament

The principal purpose of the Old Covenant was to prepare for the coming of Christ, the universal redeemer, and the messianic kingdom.

■ Chapter V: The New Testament

.... The Gospels have a special pre-eminence. They are of apostolic origin.

.... The sacred authors wrote the four Gospels, selecting some things from the many which had been handed down by word of mouth or in writing...always in such fashion that they told us the honest truth about Jesus.

■ Chapter VI: Sacred Scripture in the Life of the Church

.... The Church has always regarded the Scriptures

together with Sacred Tradition as the supreme rule of faith.

.… The Church is concerned to move ahead daily toward a deeper understanding of the Sacred Scriptures so that she may unceasingly feed her sons with the Divine Word.

…. Sacred Theology rests on the written word of God, together with Sacred Tradition, as its primary and perpetual foundation.

…. The Vatican Council earnestly and specifically urges all Christian faithful to learn by frequent reading of the divine Scriptures.

…. Ignorance of the Scriptures is ignorance of Christ.

…. Prayer should accompany the reading of Sacred Scripture, so that God and man may talk together.

…. Just as the life of the Church grows through persistent participation in the Eucharistic mystery, so may we hope for a new surge of spiritual vitality from intensified veneration for God's Word.

■ Pope Benedict XVI's Apostolic Exhortation

The most recent Catholic statement about the use of the Bible was that of Pope Benedict XVI. Following a synod of bishops who reviewed and studied the significance of the Bible in the life and the mission of the Church, on September 30, 2010, the Pope issued his Apostolic Exhortation *Verbum Domini* (Word of the Lord). The exhortation has three main parts, each with several chapters.

■ Part One

Chapter 1 – "The God who speaks," underscores God's will to open and maintain a dialog with man in which God takes the initiative and reveals himself in various ways.

Chapter 2 – "Our response to the God who speaks." Man is called to enter into alliance with his God, who listens to him in response to his questions.

Chapter 3 – "Instant interpretation of sacred Scripture in the church." The Senate reaffirmed teachings of Vatican II Dogmatic Constitution on the word of God.

■ Part Two

Chapter 1 – "The word of God and the Church."

Chapter 2 – "The Liturgy, Privileged Setting the Word of God." This talks about the vital link between sacred Scriptures and the sacraments and especially the Eucharist.

Chapter 3 – "The Word of God in the Life of the Church." This emphasizes the importance of biblical inspiration for pastoral activity and catechesis, the biblical formation of Christians, and the use of sacred Scripture in great Ecclesiastical gatherings. In this section, we find the emphasis of Pope Benedict for the laity to practice divine reading (*lectio divina*).

■ Part Three

Chapter 1 – "The Church's Mission to Proclaim the Word of God to the World." The duty of Christians is to announce the word of God in the world in which they live and work.

Chapter 2 – "The Word of God and Commitment to the World." Christians are called to serve the word of God in their most needy brothers and sisters.

Chapter 3 – "The Word of God and Culture." The Pope expresses his hope that the Bible may be better known in schools and universities and better use made of social communications media.

Chapter 4 – "The Word of God and Inter-religious Dialogue." This provides guidelines concerning dialogue between Christians and Muslims and with members of other non-Christian religions within the framework of religious liberty.

An English copy of Verbum Domini is free online.
Search for Post-Synodal Apostolic Exhortation

Pope Benedict encourages the laity to practice *lectio divina* and explains the four basic steps of this form of prayer. The first step is to open the Bible and ask the question "What does the biblical text say in itself?" Next, one enters meditation and asks "What does the biblical text say to me?" Here the individual must let himself or herself be moved and challenged. Following meditation, one enters the stage of prayer and asks, "What do we say to the Lord in response to his word?" Prayer is the primary way by which the word of God transforms us. The last step asks "What conversion of mind, heart, and life is the Lord asking of us?"

■ The Catechism of the Catholic Church

The *Catechism of the Catholic Church* makes this statement about how God reveals himself and his message:

By natural reason, man can know God with certainty, on the basis of his works. But there is another order of knowledge, which man cannot possibly arrive at by his own powers: the order of Divine Revelation. Through an utterly free decision, God has revealed himself and given himself to man. He does this by revealing the mystery, his plan of loving goodness, formed from all eternity in Christ, for the benefit of all men. God has fully revealed this plan by sending us his beloved son, Our Lord Jesus Christ and the Holy Spirit.

> For further study, consult the Catechism of the Catholic Church, Part One, Section One, Chapter Two "God comes to meet Man."

■ Catholic Interpretation of the Bible

How do we interpret the Bible? This is a question routinely asked in Bible appreciation classes. And, it is a most important question. It is asking "Just exactly how am I to understand the Bible?" Catholics who do not have a real familiarity with the Bible tend to avoid any discussion about it. When door-to-door missionaries ring the doorbell of a Catholic home, it is common for them to receive a polite but firm, "No thank you, we are Catholics and not interested." That answer does not reflect so much on a Catholic family's disinterest in the Bible, as it does on the disinterest in an interpretation of the Bible that most Catholics believe is wrong. The Catholic Church believes that the Bible is the word of God. Catholics have a profound respect for the message contained in the words of the Bible, and a deep reverence for the holiness of the Bible as divine communication with humankind.

This respect and reverence, for many Catholics, has generated an awe and fear that the Bible is best left in the hands of the leaders and teachers of the Catholic Church. Many of today's more mature Catholics will talk about how they grew up almost afraid to open the Bible. Such a feeling is justified in light of Catholic Church teaching on the Bible for centuries. Moreover, who would want the fate of some Christian splinter groups of the thirteenth, fourteenth, and fifteenth centuries who dared translate the Bible into their own languages! Being burned at the stake!

The convocation of Council of Trent was a direct reaction to the Protestant Reformation. The Protestant Reformation in large part had to do with the availability of the Bible to everyone. In this respect, the Protestant Reformation was a wonderful event for the entire Christian world. The sacred scriptures were quickly translated into the language of the people. The Bible, the word of God, came to the common man. Unfortunately, this availability of the Bible opened the doors to gross misunderstanding and misuse, stemming from the multiplicity of interpretations that arose from reading the Bible, and this has led to greater fragmentation of Christianity. Today, there are over a thousand different Christian denominations in North America. The old adage, "never argue about politics and religion" could not find greater application than "interpretation of the Bible."

The Bible in its entirety is a record of God's love for man. The Bible in its many fractured parts is a history of man's inhumanity to man.

The concept of biblical interpretation is complex and layered. This is so, not because it has developed into some precise science, but because of the awesome richness of the written word of God. In the basic view of biblical interpretation, we can see three levels, or perhaps better, distinct categories. To say levels of interpretation may give the impression of ranked importance. But each level is very important. So maybe the term category is better, since it is easier to view categories as equal rather than levels as equal. The three categories of interpretation as taught by the Catholic Church and several mainstream Protestant denominations (Lutheran, Presbyterian, Methodist, Anglican) are the: (1) literal sense of scripture, (2) the spiritual sense of scripture, and (3) the fuller sense of scripture.

The literal sense provides the meaning (and the linguistic interpretation) of the actual words of the Bible. That is, what do the words of the Bible say and what do they mean? Finding the real meaning of a scriptural passage involves not only the study of the languages that the books of the Bible were written in, but study of the literary style and forms, the social and cultural environment, the religious meaning of events and actions, and the historical situation. It is obvious there is a lot of complexity and layering in the "literal sense" of sacred Scripture.

Very important note: The "literal sense of scripture" is not the same as a "literal interpretation" of the Bible. The "literal interpretation" of Scripture, which the Catholic Church does not espouse, means taking the words of the Bible exactly as they are written and superimposing on them our modern mindset with little or no regard at all for the intent of the author, the literary genre used, the historical situation of the writing, or the primitive cosmology that prevailed at the time. Earth is not the physical center of the universe. The sun, moon, and stars are not little lights placed in an inverted dome over the flat earth.

The spiritual sense is the message we can understand when we read the Bible and see the spiritual connections between events, as one leads to another, as one provides deeper appreciation of the continuity of God's loving interest and insertion into the history of man. And, God's loving interest in the history of man did not end with the Resurrection of Jesus. Mankind is still flourishing two thousand years after Jesus Christ. The Catholic Church believes that God continues to insert himself into the history of man through and in Jesus with the guidance of the Holy Spirit. This is a continuing and living expression of faith. Scriptural interpretation is a dynamic process that is found within the Bible and continues in the life of the Church.

The fuller sense is a meaning of the scriptural text at a more profound level. This is viewed as something God intended, but not clearly expressed by the human author, before the fulfillment of other conditions. It is the Holy Spirit, the real author of the sacred scriptures, who brings out this fuller sense in the human awareness through greater prayer and meditation on the Bible and through careful, reflective study. This is a kind of "beyond the normal" sense.

For the person interested in a deeper knowledge of the "Catholic Church Interpretation of the Bible," it is indispensable to read the statement of the Pontifical Biblical Commission issued in 1992. It can easily be found on the Worldwide Web. This document explains different types of approaches to interpretation, different tools of interpretation, and the wealth and riches that these efforts bring to the study of the Word of God.

A final word about the Catholic interpretation of the Bible. In matters of interpreting the meaning of a particular part of the Bible, the Catholic faithful will always defer to the teaching authority of the Church, which is also called the *Magisterium*. In matters of faith and morals, the Magisterium is our guide. And that is common sense. Few members of the Catholic laity are in the business of proclaiming and defining church doctrine. Deferring to the Magisterium in matters of faith and morals is not the same thing as private reading of the Bible and arriving at a deeper understanding and spiritual appreciation. The Catholic layperson has every right to read the Bible and freely discuss what she or he derives from that reading. Greater familiarity with the Bible through daily reading and better understanding of the Bible through study, will give you a more solid basis for intelligently discussing and expressing your own views without fear of grievous sin.

■ Inspiration and Inerrancy in the Bible

Two terms that come up sooner or later in anyone's dealings with the Bible are "inspiration" and "inerrancy." These are two very important, but not easily definable, terms. Perhaps we accept both concepts because they make sense, whether or not we can fully and lucidly articulate what they are. Our faith and basic intelligence tell us that if Almighty God wants to communicate with us in some written fashion, he will do so in one or more of the human languages that we can understand.

From our own experience, we know that God communicates with us. This may be in our heart, in our conscience, or in our intellect. Either way, it is a kind of inspiration. Inspiration, in its most basic sense, means to inject or be injected with the spirit. The whisperings of our hearts, the probing of our consciences, the enlightenment of our minds, all come from that unseen force that fills the universe with love, judgment, courage, compassion, understanding, and creativity. Deep in our souls we know that God inspires. And the Supreme Goodness and Truth will inspire those chosen to put God's communications down in pen and ink to do so without any divine error.

The Catholic Church, like all Christian churches, denominations and sects, teaches that Bible is the inspired word of God. Even though our hearts guide us to this reality, we may still have questions. Just what is this inspiration? How did God inspire the Bible? How did God inspire the men or women who wrote the Bible? How far does God's inspiration go?…to the person who put down the words?…to the person or persons who revised and redacted the scripture?….to that group of people or religious council that decided which books of scripture would be included on the official list, or Canon?…to the people who translated the Bible to other languages?

The Catholic Church teaches that the Bible is without error. One of the fundamental qualities of the Bible is "inerrancy," there is no error in it. Again, our hearts tell us that God will not deceive us. But we still have questions. We ask…what kind of error are we talking about? Contradictions are easy to find in the Bible. Scientific errors are easy to find in the Bible. Historical inaccuracies are easy to find in the Bible. All this might make you ask, "What definition of error are we using when we claim that the Bible is without error?" Not an easy question to answer intelligently and intelligibly. Some attempt an answer by saying "Every word in the Bible is inspired by God, so every word is true. Therefore we must believe every word as we see it. Inerrancy means that there is no error in the Bible…anywhere." People who espouse this level of inerrancy have to totally close their eyes to what they see around them. Maybe this is an expression of a total trust and confidence in God. Maybe it is a kind of myopia that some people must deal with. The Catholic Church does not espouse this approach or view of inerrancy. Basically, the Catholic Church accepts that there is human error in the Bible, but no error in God's divine message that is communicated through the Bible.

The Catholic Church has always believed and taught that God inspired the Bible. The *Constitution on Divine Revelation* from the Vatican II dedicated a section on inspiration of the Bible. This is in chapter III. That is the best place to go to find out what the Catholic Church is teaching on this topic. The basic idea is that God chose certain people to compose sacred writings and in some way guided them to convey the message God wanted man to know. The people chosen, however, used their own abilities and talents in the composition, and they were limited by and influenced by the circumstances of their lives. The way they saw the world is the way they expressed it in their writing. The way they perceived events and actions is the way they wrote them. Yet despite these limitations, God acted through them in some special way so that the Bible writers put down on paper what God wanted them to write.

What the Catholic Church does not believe and teach about inspiration, is that it means some kind of "divine dictation" where the designated "inspired" person is an instrument that mechanically or blindly wrote the exact words that were given to him by some spirit source.

Inerrancy is similar to the idea of inspiration. It all has to do with God's will. The Bible is free of divine error; however, it is clearly not free of human error. This can get complicated if we let it. But it won't if we recognize that God's being is so far above our being, and His will and providence are so infinitely superior to anything we can imagine. Listen to the heart and know God is there.

■ Deuterocanonical Books, Apocrypha and the Canon

Several terms that will come up when you're looking more deeply at the numerous books making up the Old Testament and the New Testament are "canon," "apocrypha," and "deuterocanonical." Canon refers to the correct list of authentic books that comprise the Holy Scriptures, or the Bible. Apocrypha refers to books that have biblical themes, but are not accepted as part of the collection of books that make up the accepted Bible. And, deuterocanonical refers to a certain group of books with biblical themes that were not part of the Jewish scriptures written in Hebrew, but were part of the Jewish scriptures written in

Greek. Deuterocanonical is a term used by the Catholic Church, but generally not used by Protestants.

The difference between the Catholic Bible and the Protestant Bible is the Catholic Church's acceptance of deuterocanonical books as authentic writings that should be accepted as belonging to the Canon of Sacred Scripture. In the earlier section of this book "Catholic Bible and Protestant Bible," a list compares the books the Catholic Bible and those of the Protestant Bible. As you may recall, the Catholic Bible has seven more books in the Old Testament than the Protestant Bible.

The term apocrypha, as used by Protestant churches, applies to a list of fifteen books which they do not believe belong in the canon. Seven of these books that the Catholic Church accepts as deuterocanonical are listed as apocrypha in Protestant bibles. The variance between the Catholic Canon and the Protestant Canon goes back to the difference between the Jewish scriptures written in Hebrew and the Jewish scriptures written in Greek.

A brief look at the development of the Jewish Bible shows that the holy books were written in Hebrew while the people were together as a nation in one common territory (even when the kingdom was divided). The destruction of the Northern Kingdom by the Assyrians in eighth century B.C., through the destruction of the Southern Kingdom by the Babylonians in the sixth century B.C., initiated a great geographical dispersion of the people away from their Promised Land. The struggle of Israel and Judah against the Assyrians and later the Babylonians, ended in a great loss of life and the final deportation into exile. This resulted in the Jewish people settling in foreign lands, and through many generations, adapting to the common languages of the times, Aramaic and Greek. During the third and second century B.C, the Jewish Scriptures were translated into Greek. Known today as the Septuagint, this Greek translation became the standard Bible for the

Greek-speaking Jews. The collection of holy books that the Greek-speaking Jews included in the Septuagint listed the seven books of Tobit, Judith, Wisdom, Sirach, Baruch, 1 and 2 Maccabees, along with the thirty-nine books of the Hebrew Old Testament. When the first major Christian translation of Jewish Sacred Scriptures into Latin occurred, the Greek Septuagint version was used, and the additional seven books became part of the Christian Bible.

Later in time, when the Church defined the canon of the Bible, it contained forty-six canonical (authentic) books in the Old Testament. It differentiated the canonical status of the thirty-nine books in the Hebrew Bible and the seven additional books of the Greek Bible, as being authentic books of the first Canon and the authentic books of the second Canon.

For the Catholic Church, the term deuterocanonical refers to these seven books. The prefix "*deutero*" comes from the Greek word meaning second or after. The seven deuterocanonical books in the Catholic Bible were accepted as authentic at a later time. The first group of thirty-nine books is referred to as the "protocanonical" books. The prefix proto-, also from Greek, means first or before. So the thirty-nine protocanonical books came first, but were not any more divinely inspired than the deuterocanonical books. For the Catholic Church, protocanonical books and deuterocanonical books are equally inspired by God and equally revered by Catholics. That is why Catholic bibles have forty-six books of the Old Testament.

The term apocrypha refers to a number books of uncertain or questionable origin which claim to be divinely inspired. Many modern day versions of the Protestant Bible include these apocryphal books as an addendum to the Bible. Protestants do not accept the terms protocanonical and deuterocanonical. For them, any book claiming divine origin that is not on the list of thirty-nine is considered apocrypha.

As may be realized, this difference between the Catholic and Protestant bibles can cause considerable controversy for anyone interested in argument, and especially for people who are bent on proselytizing. Where it does generate polemic and proselytizing, it seems like the whole message in the Bible of God's love is completely missed.

The seven deuterocanonical books for the Catholic Church there are:

Tobit	Baruch
Judith	1 Maccabees
Wisdom	2 Maccabees
Sirach	

The fourteen books Protestant churches consider apocrypha follow:

Tobit	1st Esdras
Judith	2nd Esdras
Wisdom	Parts of Daniel
Sirach	Parts of Lamentations
Baruch	Parts of Esther
1 Maccabees	3 Maccabees
2 Maccabees	4 Maccabees

Bible Appreciation Quiz for Chapter VIII

What do you know about the Catholic Church Teaching on the Bible?

(1.) When did Pope Benedict XIII promulgate his encyclical on the Bible, *Providentissimus Deus*?

_____

(2.) What is the name of the document of Vatican II that explains doctrine of the Bible?

_____

(3.) What is the title of Pope Benedict XVI's Apostolic Exhortation on the Holy Scriptures?

_____

(4.) What are the three categories of biblical interpretation?

_____

(5.) What is the *Magisterium* of the Catholic Church?

_____

(6.) What does the term "deuterocanonical" refer to?

_____

(7.) What is the Protestant term for "deuterocanonical?"

_____

Chapter IX: Other Comments on the Bible

■Author and Genius of the Bible

As we get more and more into reading, studying, and praying the Bible, the experience of "awesome" becomes inescapable. The Bible is truly amazing. This value can be lost or obscured in the sheer volume of Bibles in the world. Bibles are so commonplace; they are sold everywhere: in church lobbies (vestibules!), religious bookstores; general bookstores, religious goods and religious articles shops; department stores, corner drugstores, supermarkets, airports, flea markets, and by door- to-door salespeople. The Bible is the single most produced book in history in hardback, paperback, electronic media, and audio tapes. And, you do not have to purchase one. Free Bibles are available from many sources: groups, associations, and Bible societies like the famous Gideon's that place Bibles generously and virtually in any location where a person might spend the night, or stop for a period of rest and personal reflection. With such a business that has gone on unchecked and un-audited for centuries, one wonders how much the author(s) receives in royalties each year!

It appears utterly ridiculous to make such a statement like "the Bible is a great work of inspired genius." That is almost universally acclaimed!

The Bible is one integral book and at the same time the Bible is an anthology of many different pieces of writing and literature. As far as the Bible being one integral book, the Holy Spirit was actively engaged for a period of about 1,500 years, inspiring individuals and guiding groups in the process of writing, editing, and selecting specific holy writings and culminating the work into a final fixed canon. That there were many holy books written under the inspiration of the Holy Spirit cannot be reasonably contested. Starting in the first pages of the Bible, we see clear evidence of several different sources and traditions about the beginning of the world and the origins of humanity. The first and easiest demonstration of this comes from two differing explanations of how the world was created and the sequence of events that occurred. Chapter 1 in Genesis gives us the well-known "seven-day" creation event. The second chapter in Genesis, beginning in verse 4, gives the reader a reverse order of the sequence and reasons for the existence of mankind and animal kind. The choice of words and names and terminology found in the first five books of the Bible (the *Pentateuch* of Christian Bibles and the *Torah* of Jewish Scripture) also demonstrate that the various books of the Bible were not written by one individual, especially in the final form we read today.

Scholarly study and investigation both by Protestant and Catholic biblical experts, delve into deeper aspects and elements of the Bible books that point to many elements coming from multiple sources that are found in what we traditionally consider one book by one person. In the book of the Old Testament prophet Daniel, for example, the person and place of Daniel is in Babylon during the Babylonian Exile under kings Nebuchadnezzar and Balthazar, a period from 586 B.C. to 538

B.C. There are major elements in Daniel that requires knowledge of events around 400 B.C. If Daniel wrote the entire book, he lived to be quite an old man.

As an integral book, the Bible is brilliantly crafted with a prologue (see Genesis 1–11) that begins before known time and history, and provides us with divine principles and eternal messages, passes through nearly two thousand years of human history and preparation for and witness to the ultimate and perfect revelation of God to mankind, and ends with an epilogue (Revelation) which is beyond known time and reconfirms the divine principles and messages of the prologue. What are those divine realities? That God, not man, is in charge in the beginning, and God, not man, is in charge at the end; that man rebelled against God in the beginning, and man continues to rebel against God unto the end; that in the beginning God promised a savior who would right the wrongs of man's rebelliousness and that God fulfilled that promise through the incarnation of His only begotten eternal Son.

■ Holy Books and the Bible

The Bible is the Holy Book of hundreds of millions of people in the world.

Other special books that reach additional millions include:

Islam	Koran	by Mohammed
Hinduism	Upanishads	by 20,000 or more
Confucianism	Classic of Filial Piety	by Confucius
Taoism	Book of Tao	by Lao Tse

Catholics should respect the rights of believers in the non-Christian religions of the world and, as such, respect their holy books. Although it has been on the back-burner in recent decades, nearly 50 years ago, the Vatican II acknowledged freedom of religion to people of the world. "The Church rejects, as foreign to the mind of Christ, any discrimination against men or harassment of them because of their race, color, condition of life or religion...The Catholic Church rejects nothing which is true and holy in these religions."

Vatican II encouraged dialogue with followers of other religions and to "...acknowledge and promote the spiritual and moral goods found among these men, well as the values in their society and culture."

Source: Vatican II "Declaration on the Relationship of the Church to Non-Christian Religions" and "Declaration on Religious Freedom." www.vatican.va/archive

"It is not for us to pass precise judgments on the elements of sin or satanic evil which may also be found in these forms of thought. Hinduism and Buddhism set men's minds own Nirvana. Islamic doctrine demands that all men must call God father. Humanism teaches children not to turn to God. Marxism holds out a future that will never come. There is some wickedness and corruption in all this. But we must trust in the spirit of God, who leaves no man untouched, and concentrate on the truth and goodness which they offer to men."

[*The New Catechism*, pg.33, Herder and Herder, New York, 1967.]

■ Uniqueness of Bible among These Great Religious Books

The Christian Bible is a single collection, of many sources, not written by one person, but possessing a remarkable unity of many authors. Catholics believe the one real author is the Holy Spirit, who worked through many human "contributing" authors.

■ Surrounded in Mystery?

Many Catholics say they find the Bible hard to understand. That feeling can be appreciated. It is hard to understand if you don't have much of an idea of what it is about. But unfortunately, many Catholics are satisfied with this situation, that because the Bible is hard to understand, it can be left alone. Such a decision results in a profound loss.

"The reader can easily be very bewildered by it. Possibly he expects a pious and edifying book, that is, moralizing writing which does no more than put virtuous deeds before us. But the story of the patriarchs already contains a number of crude and savage deeds or things that we find immoral, all told quite dispassionately. The reader has then to admit that the Bible is not a 'pious' book, but the echo of reality, as God joins a very primitive humanity on its March."

[*The New Catechism*, pg.57]

Not knowing about the Bible, not reading the Bible, is like walking along a mountain trail casually picking up rocks and stones and tossing them down into the ravine...not knowing you are tossing away diamonds. The Holy Spirit spent about two thousand years writing, revising, adding, deleting, editing and polishing the priceless jewel we call the Bible. All this effort has been given to us as a beautiful written record of God's untiring love for us. What does the Holy Spirit think when we say, "Naw, it's too hard to understand," before we even open the Bible?

The mystery of the Bible is not difficult to dispel. Learning a few fundamentals, observing a few guidelines, following a path, and praying to the Holy Spirit, will enable you to enjoy the endless treasure of God's written revelation.

■ God of Justice, God of Love

We frequently hear that the image of God in the Old Testament is a God of justice and that the image of God in the New Testament is a God of love. And, certainly, there is no way the God in the Old Testament can compare with the God of love demonstrated in the New Testament. There are enough episodes of God's justice and wrath expressed in the Old Testament, beginning with the expulsion of Adam and Eve from the Garden of Eden and through the history of Israel until the Babylonian Exile, which occurred because of man's infidelity. Compare this with the New Testament, and the Old Testament does seem to present more an image of a God of justice. That image deserves a second look.

An enduring message of the Old Testament is definitely one of love. It is found throughout the Old Testament. But sometimes the message is disguised. Word choices in translating the Bible obviously demand an expert knowledge of the languages in which they were written. In older English translations of the Bible you can find words like "charity" and "mercy" instead of "love." Then again, languages change with time; words take on different meanings and nuances. Today, charity means helping the poor, almsgiving, and acts of good will.

To express God's infinite and perfect love, different versions of the Bible use different vocabulary, but they mean the same:

Mercy	"His mercy endures forever."
Everlasting love	"His everlasting love endures forever."
Steadfast love	"His steadfast love endures forever."
Faithful love	"His faithful love endures forever."

God's love is a very description of who and what God is. To portray the depth of this wonderful love, the words mercy, everlasting love, steadfast love, or faithful love, are used hundreds of times throughout the Old Testament. Does that tell us something? God's love is everywhere. In the Old Testament, God's love is also found everywhere. God's love teaches mankind what love is.

In the creation story, God demonstrates his goodness and goes out beyond himself to share his being and life with another.

With the Patriarchs, we see God caring and nourishing, and the patriarchs' recognition of God's steadfast love. Isaac and Rebecca (Gen 24:14 & 27) "Blessed be the Lord, the God of my master Abraham, who has not forsaken his steadfast love and his faithfulness towards my master." Jacob (Genesis 32:9 – 10) "O God of my father Abraham and the God of my father Isaac, O Lord who didst say to me 'return to your country and to your kindred and I will do you good,' I am not worthy of the least of all the steadfast love in all the faithfulness which thou has shown to thy servant." Joseph, when he was in prison, "the Lord was with Joseph and showed him steadfast love."

In the Exodus, God did marvels to bring the Hebrews out of slavery, and later, in the desert, Moses received the ten commandments for a second time (Ex 34:6–7). "The Lord, the Lord, a God merciful and gracious, slow to anger, and abounding in steadfast love and faithfulness, keeping steadfast love for thousands."

In Deuteronomy, Moses teaches his people, "Know therefore that the Lord your God is God, the faithful God who keeps covenant and steadfast love with those who love him and keep his commandments, to a thousand generations." (Dt 7:9)

In the historical books, the stories both of God's steadfast love and the Israelites' unfaithfulness to God: 2 Sam 15:20; 1 Kgs 8:23, "God of Israel there is no God like thee, in heaven above our own earth beneath, keeping covenant and showing steadfast love to thy servants who walk before thee with all their heart." In 2 Chr 20:21, "Give thanks to the Lord, for his steadfast love endures forever."

In the prophetical books one reads, many times the prophets reminded the Israelites of God's unfailing love. No matter what happens, God is there with open arms. Isaiah (Is 54:10). God's message through Isaiah, "for the mountains may depart and the hills be removed, but my steadfast love shall not depart from you, and my covenant of peace shall not be removed."

The prophet Hosea in word and action with his unfaithful wife, Gomer, graphically illustrates the profound love of God toward the constantly unfaithful Israelites. "And, I will betroth you to me forever; I will betroth you to me in righteousness and in justice, in steadfast love, and then mercy."(Hos 2:19)

And finally, the Psalms. Forty-seven psalms speak of God's steadfast love. If you are still not convinced about God's steadfast love in the Old Testament, go to Appendix B near the end of this book, and you'll find the list of the forty-seven psalms.

Comparing the two images "a God of justice" and "a God of love" in the Old Testament, God of justice seems to come in second.

■ The Human Side of the Bible

The general Catholic view is that the Bible is indisputably the word of God. At the same time, the Bible is indisputably words of men. The word of God concept does not cause us problems; however, the words of men can cause major problems.

Many Catholics are "turned off" when they begin reading the Bible because of what they view as very unchristian events, actions, and sentiments. In these objectionable stories, to God is attributed the order or directive for deceit, lying, stealing, killing, revenge, vindictiveness, inhumanity. It is reported in the Bible that the Lord God ordered slaughters, massacres, and pillaging. And, putting it mildly, these things clash with the concept of a loving God.

The Vatican II *Constitution on Divine Revelation*, as discussed earlier, recognized the human element in the words of Holy Scripture. Chapter III clearly states the Church's official understanding of the role of the Holy Spirit and the role of the human writers in preparing the written Scriptures.

The people who wrote the books of the Bible were no less human or more super human than anyone else. Just as people of the twenty-first century are affected and influenced by many things, factors, conditions, and forces, so were the human contributors to the earthly rendition of the Divine message to the inhabitants of this planet.

The final judgment on this human side of the Bible, however, is not ours to make. It may appear wrong and not God's way…and that might be correct. But then, we do not know God's ways. His thoughts are not our thoughts, and his ways are not our ways. How inscrutable are the thoughts of God!

As far as definitive pronouncements of the Catholic Church on these human elements are concerned, there are none that the Catholic faithful are obliged to accept. The official teaching prudently defers to a later time when, maybe the Holy Spirit will make things clearer. Submission to God's will is the basis to the fulfillment of our being. Jesus is the yardstick for Christian living. In the end, it is always "Thy will be done" followed by "into thy hands I commend my spirit."

The Old Testament is not Christian. It is Jewish, not of our contemporary times, but from 2,500 years or more in the past. No teachings of Jesus proclaim, or even suggest, the brutal slaughter of men, women, and children found in the Old Testament books of Numbers, Deuteronomy, Joshua, Judges, and …not even when it is done in God's name. Jesus had legions of angels that could have come to his assistance, that could have wrought fearsome vengeance, but he did not ask for any. The Old Testament provides some of the basic ingredients, vital to the preparation for the New Testament. Knowledge of this preparation is valuable for a fuller understanding and appreciation of God's insertion into human history.

We cannot judge the people of the Old Testament. We cannot compare our lives to theirs, our customs to their customs. If a person lives by the best information available at that time, then that is God's will. No one can do any better. People 500 or 1,000 years from now will surely see things to criticize about the twenty-first century people in the beginning of the new Millennium. "How could those people think that way? How could those people do those things? How could some nations ignore such massive suffering of fellow human beings?" Would we want viewers from the future to look back and consider us insensitive to our fellow human beings, careless with our natural resources, or ignorant of global realities and needs?

■ Women in the Old Testament

The Bible is a central part of our faith, and we look to it to help us understand more about our faith, and to provide us with insights and guide us on the road we are traveling. The Old Testament records almost two thousand years of God's personal dealings with humankind. Through it we come to learn and comprehend God's loving plan of salvation.

The people of the Old Testament were undeniably patriarchal. The books of the Bible were written by people whose social and cultural experiences and mindset were patriarchal. The story of the Old Testament readily strikes the modern reader as being extremely one-sided and not a little misogynistic. With a few exceptions, all the leaders were men, the prophets were men, the royal leaders were men, the religious leaders were men, the teachers were men, the thinkers were men, and the poets were men. For the most part, women were secondary in the major current of the history of the chosen people of the Old Testament.

To demonstrate the patriarchal character of the Old Testament and the secondary role of women, make a comparison. Off the top of your head, how many men of the Old Testament can you name? Adam, Cain, Abel, Methuselah, Noah, Abraham, Isaac, Jacob, Joseph, Moses, Aaron, Joshua, Elijah, Samuel, David, Solomon, Isaiah, Jeremiah, Ezekiel, Daniel, Jonah, and many more. Right? Now, off the top of your head, how many women of the Old Testament can you name? Eve, Sarah, Rachel, Rebecca…Deborah…Delilah…Jezebel. The names of women are more difficult to recall.

Seth was the third son of Adam and Eve. He was a good man. He married and had a son named Enosh. Seth lived 912 years and fathered many sons and daughters. Did Seth's wife live 900 years? How many times did she give birth to sons and daughters? What was her name? Seth's wife's name was never mentioned.

One of the best known stories of the Old Testament is Noah and the Flood. Noah had three sons: Shem, Ham, and Japheth. What was the name of Noah's wife? Her name was not mentioned.

Several dozen women are named in the Old Testament. Most frequently, though not exclusively, the role of women throughout the Old Testament is that of wife and mother. Those are beautiful, worthy, and necessary roles, but the Old Testament does not dwell much on those values. The "movers and shakers" of the Old Testament were men. The heroes and villains were men. And, in a patriarchal mentality that was to be expected.

The damaging and pernicious element in the Old Testament is the use of a misogynistic stereotype that is woven through the fabric of the written record of God's early dealings with humankind. This aspect of the human element and influence in the authorship of the books of the Bible can easily lead the impetuous reader to quickly throw the Bible in the trash can.

Very early on in the Bible story women reveal their undesirable characteristics. In Genesis, we see Eve: a helpmate, but ambitious and easily deceived, who drags man down into sin [see Gen 3:1–20]. Sarah was envious and hateful of her maidservant Hagar whom she had given as a wife to Abraham. Women use their sexual attractiveness to lure men into bad decisions and sinful actions, as seen in the episode of Genesis where the unnamed wife of Potiphar, a high-ranking official in Egypt, tried to seduce the handsome young Joseph [see Gen 39:7–20]. Wives and mothers (Rebecca) used deceit to further their own goals and desires [see Gen 27:1–40].

Bible Appreciation Quiz for Chapter IX – Women 1

Are you familiar with these women? What did they do to earn a mention in the Bible?

Eve, Gen 2–7

_____

Adah, Gen 4:20

_____

Bilhah, Gen 29–30; 37

_____

Zipporah, Ex 2; 4

_____

Sarah, Gen 12–15

_____

Leah, Gen 29–35

_____

Miriam, Ex 15

Rebecca, Gen 22–27

Zilpah, Gen 30; 35

Zillah, Gen 4:20

Jochebed, Nb 26

Rachel, Gen 29–35

Asenath, Gen 41:46

Ruth, Rt 1–4

In the pejorative images of the Old Testament, women come across as complaining, whimpering, deceiving, weak and helpless, and often as filthy prostitutes. The great prophet Jeremiah disparages the image of womanhood, by using the example of the prostitute to describe the unfaithfulness of Israel [Je 2:30; 3:1; 13:26–27]. Israel forsook its covenant with the Lord. Ezekiel preached at length about the prostitute Israel [Ez 16:15–30].

Women were also the object of men's pleasure. Men who could afford more than one woman readily took all they could manage. As often as not, man was not able to manage the multiplicity very well. Jealous wives and concubines manipulated their men and persuaded them to do all sorts of things, but the worst evil of all was to draw a man away from his focus on God. Eve started the ball rolling, and it was downhill ever after. Solomon's many women debilitated his great wisdom and initiated several hundred years of sinfulness, idolatry, and unfaithfulness to the God of Israel and the God of Judah.

Feminine beauty was an esteemed characteristic, and could be used to achieve a variety of ends, admirable or otherwise. Jael lured Sisera, commander of the army of the king of Canaan, into her tent where she hosted him, and then assassinated him. Delilah, the beautiful and seductive Philistine, deceived Samson and delivered him into the hands of the Philistine army. Judith, a beautiful and daring Jewess, used her grace and charm to gain access to the enemy general, Holofernes, and decapitated him. Esther was put in beauty treatment and training for a year so she could win a contest and gain the king's eye to become queen of Babylonia!

Bible Appreciation Quiz for
Chapter IX – Women -2

How many women of the Old Testament are you familiar with? What did they do to earn a mention in the Old Testament?

Rahah, Jos 2, 6

_____

Abigail, 1 Sam 25, 27

_____

Deborah, g 4–5

_____

Bathsheba, 2 Sam 11–12

_____

Delilah, Jg 16

_____

Jezebel, 1 Kg 16–21

_____

Hannah, 1 Sam 1–2

_____

Judith, Book of Judith

_____

Ahinoam, 1 Sam 25, 27

_____

Esther, Book of Esther

_____

The New Testament presents women differently. Whereas there is not a lot about women in the New Testament, we do not find any episodes where women are presented in an unsavory manner. In the four Gospels, the women mentioned came in contact with Jesus Christ in some way: mother, friend, follower, a person seeking healing, or a Samaritan villager giving water to a stranger. In Acts of the Apostles and Paul's Epistles, women are sometimes recorded as leaders in their communities.

Bible Appreciation Quiz for Chapter IX – Women 3

How many women of the New Testament are you familiar with?

Who were they, and what did they do to earn a mention in the New Testament?

Anna, Lk 2

_____

Apphia, Ph 1

_____

Bernice, Act 25

_____

Chloe, 1 Cor 1

_____

Claudia, 2 Tim 4

_____

Dorcas, Act 9

_____

Elizabeth, Lk 1

_____

Joanna, Lk 24

_____

Lydia, Act 1

_____

Herodias, Mt 14; Mk 6

_____

Mary, Mother of Jesus, Lk 1

_____

Mary Magdalene, Jn 19; Lk 8; Mk 15; Mt 27

_____

Mary, Mk 15

_____

Martha, Lk 10

_____

Prisca, Act 18

Salome, Mk 15

Sapphira, Act 5

Tabitha, Act 9

Tryphaena, Rm 16

Tryphosa, Rm 16

An understanding and appreciation of the human element in the Bible is vital for every Bible reader, but more so for those who might be turned off by the images in the Old Testament.

■ BA and Catholic Spirituality

The goal of *Bible Appreciation for Catholics* is to help Catholics bridge the gap in biblical knowledge between Catholics and other Christian denominations. Since the time of the Protestant Reformation, which began in the 1500s, Protestant Christians have laid claim to the Bible, so much so that for almost five centuries, the Catholic laity has hardly opened the Bible. This is not to accuse Catholics of ignoring or disrespecting the Bible. Catholics hold the Bible in awe. However, there is a legacy of fear about the Bible. This, too, comes from the time of the Protestant Reformation, not from Protestantism itself, but from the Catholic Church and its "Counter-Reformation" effort, that powerfully proclaimed and promulgated by the Council of Trent, which convened from 1545 to 1563. The Council decreed that a Latin version of the Bible, the Latin vulgate of St. Jerome, was the official Bible for Catholics and for all public use of the Bible. That effectively put the Bible out of reach for most of the Catholic laity, because they could not speak or read Latin. Additionally, the Council documents recorded… "the council decrees that no one should dare to rely on his own judgment in matters of faith and morals affecting the structure of Christian doctrine and to distort the sacred scriptures…nor should anyone dare to interpret sacred Scripture contrary to the unanimous agreement of the Fathers…."

[Source: *The Church Teaches, Documents of the Church in English,* the Council of Trent 1545–63," pp. 44–46.]

Small wonder the Catholic layperson has steered clear of the Bible!

As the years wore on following the adjournment of the Council of Trent, Catholic spirituality for the laity focused on the sacraments and devotions. Private reading of the Bible was almost a dangerous spiritual activity. The only familiarity with the Bible came from traditional Bible stories, and hearing the Gospels and Epistles read at Mass. Even now, this pattern is noticeable among the laity of the Catholic Church.

The sacraments of the Holy Eucharist and Penance, as they were commonly known, had the greatest liturgical impact on Catholic spirituality. Public and private devotional activity such as holy hours, the rosary, Benediction and Exposition of the Blessed Sacrament, novenas, prayer books, and spiritual reading, offered Catholics many avenues of growth in the spiritual life. Hundreds of canonized saints, and thousands of unrecognized saintly people prospered spiritually in this environment, as do they still today in the twenty-first century. Many Catholics today are spiritually nourished without touching the Bible. When inviting people to read the Bible or study the Bible one frequently receives a polite and sincere "I go to church every Sunday, and receive the Body of Christ; I say my prayers morning and night. I don't feel a need to read the Bible." And that is fine.

The great emphasis Protestant churches have placed on the Bible, and the wonderful apostolic energy they have demonstrated with their Bible-based spirituality, has served as an example for Catholics. In fact, the last decades of the twentieth century, the Catholic Church saw a growth in Bible study, and interest in the Bible has gradually spread. In the United States today, probably every parish has a Bible study group. But even with this growth and interest, the vast majority of Catholics do not read the Bible.

Bible Appreciation for Catholics, attempts to "bridge the 450-year gap" in biblical awareness and understanding, is also an attempt to open up and promote a great Christian treasure, to reintroduce the entirety of Sacred Scripture into the spiritual life of Catholics. Personal reading of the Bible engages the individual in a special encounter with the Holy Spirit. Extensive reading, praying, and reflecting on passages of the Bible will bring the Catholic into a greater appreciation of the

Christian faith, a strengthening of the will, and a deeper maturity and commitment as a member of the mystical body of Christ.

A brief summary of the goals of *Bible Appreciation for Catholics* is the 3 **L**s: **l**earn the Bible, **l**ove the Bible, **l**ive the Bible. It can be a compass pointing the right course through the terrain of spirituality. For a Catholic, growth in the Bible, together with the Eucharist and the treasure trove of Catholic devotions, spiritual enrichment can reach ever higher.

Learn the Bible is the individual using self-discipline to make the effort and take the time to read the Bible regularly, not just once from cover to cover, but numerous times to really learn the content of the Bible. **Love** the Bible is a result of learning the Bible and knowing it better. Like love for another person, love of the Bible grows more with time and enrichment, bringing the person to really look forward to the time of being with the Bible. Inspiration and insight into the profundity of God's written word grows as this love begins a transformation in the individual's life. God's essence, God's being in Love. Living in love is the third level or goal of Bible appreciation: **Live** the Bible.

■ Psalms and Catholic Prayer

Psalms are poems of the Hebrew people since at least the time of King David. They are some of the more well-known parts of the Bible. Recalling that David reigned about 1000 B.C., the Jewish people today still pray the psalms continuing a spiritual tradition for about three thousand years! King David is the traditional composer of these beautiful poetic prayers, and whereas a number of them were actually written by him, many were not. The non-Davidic psalms were written by unknown persons and collected over hundreds of years. This collection of poems as we have it today reached its final state after the Babylonian captivity,

600 years after King David. The early Christian church adopted the same prayers. There are 150 psalms in the Christian Bible.

The word "psalm" has its own history. It was not a Hebrew word. It came from the Greek word *psalmos,* which originally meant music of a stringed instrument. By the time of the translation of Hebrew Bible into Greek, the Septuagint, in the second century B.C., the meaning of the word *psalmos* had morphed into "songs of praise." And that was it. The collection of 150 Hebrew poems has universally come to be known as *The Psalms.*

Psalms can be classified in various categories. There are psalms intended for individuals and those intended for the community. There are royal psalms that refer to a king and what he has done. There are psalms of praise, thanksgiving, and lamentation. There are penitential psalms and pleas of help against the enemy.

In addition to the psalms, the Bible has other hymns and songs, found in different books of the Bible. A song may be one of praise, thanksgiving, and even victory. To mention some, there are the songs of: Moses [Ex 15:1–18], Deborah and Barak [Jg 5:1–31], David [1 Chron 29:1–13], the three young men in the furnace [Dan 3:57–88], Tobit [Tob 13:1–10], Judith [Jdt 16:15-21]

Becoming familiar with the psalms and understanding them in the contexts in which they were written offers Catholics a new dimension in their spiritual life. As one writer put it, "Perhaps the fresh and direct voice of the psalms is more rapidly perceived when their strangeness and antiquity has been recognized."

[Christopher Barth, *Introduction to the Psalms*, 1966]

■ Psalms in the Daily Life of the Church

The formal recitation of Psalms is a very long tradition in the Catholic Church going back to at least 230 A.D. with monastic life

(St. Hippolytus). The Psalter is an arrangement of Psalms—somewhat thematically—prayed daily at different times—referred to as the "hours." The official daily prayer of the Catholic Church consists of praying these hours. The Anglican Church and other Christian denominations also pray the Psalter. Today, there are eight periods of prayer or eight "canonical hours" stretched throughout the day. In the Catholic Church, the official prayer book of canonical hours is called the "Breviary." These canonical hours together with the daily celebration of the Eucharist constitute the public prayer life of the entire Catholic Church all around the world, east and west, north and south. It is like a mantle of prayer that envelops the earth every day in adoration, praise, and petition. This public prayer of the church, together with private prayer and devotions of individual Christians demonstrate the commitment and duty of the Church to pray constantly without ceasing.

The Pastoral Constitution on the Church in the Modern World from the Vatican II begins with the words, "The joys and hopes, the fears and anxieties of this present world are the joys and hopes, the fears and anxieties of the church...." The prayers of the church are for the world, the Kingdom of God, for all people and all things, everywhere. We often hear, especially in desperate or trying situations, "all we can do is pray." It is prayer that the Catholic Church has been doing for two thousand years. There is a timeless struggle between the human ego and the divine will, a constant clash between self-love that is focused inward and true love that is directed outward. So yes, many times it is quite true, all we can do is pray.

In the introduction to the English version of the Roman Breviary used in the United States, one reads of this total involvement of the church sharing the life and problems of the world through prayer and actions.

"The Church weeps through our tears, together with those who weep, rejoices through our joys together with those who rejoice, does penance with the penitent. All the sentiments of Holy Mother Church find their echo in our heart."

Through recital of the breviary in its entirety or in part, Catholics everywhere can participate in the Church's worldwide ministry of prayer and concern.

A person can purchase a version of the complete breviary, or a shortened form of the canonical hours, and pray with the global church. The complete breviary is an awesome treasury of prayers, psalms, meditations, sermons, homilies, and hymns that have been selected from the Church's heritage.

Sadly, the busy modern lifestyle takes people away from prayer. Many Catholics have lost the connection with the duty of prayer in and with the Church Universal. A reawakening of this duty through reading sacred Scripture and recital of the prayer of the Church could go a long way in clarifying the identity of being Catholic and revitalizing the spiritual life of the Church.

■ "I have read the Bible"

In talking about the Bible, I find Catholics who have read the entire Bible, but they did not find it very interesting because they already knew all the stories and how they ended. Others who have read the entire Bible, found it tedious and boring and with little to offer the modern mind. Still others who have read the Bible felt they did not get much out of it and preferred other more substantial spiritual books.

It is sad when someone has read the entire Bible, and the book has been placed on the bookshelf never to be opened again. Reading the entire Bible once is something of an achievement, and the first major step in learning the Bible. But, if reading it as just another book that people can say they have read, it is akin to learning their catechism to make First Communion, and then not studying any more about their Catholic faith. And, it's an understatement to say there are many Catholic adults who do not have an adult knowledge and understanding of their Catholic faith.

This brings up another matter to look at. The Bible is a very special book—Catholic belief is that the Bible was inspired by the Holy Spirit—it is God's word to man. The more you read the Bible, the more you can get out of it. The more you get out of it, the more you want to read. The growing result is that you enter into a new level of spirituality. The Bible is not just a book to be read, it is a book that is to be delved into. The author of the Bible is the Holy Spirit. Praying to the Holy Spirit is a crucial step in reading and studying the Bible. People who prayerfully read the Bible will often tell you that each time they read the Bible they learn something new or gain an insight they never had before. They experience the assistance of the Holy Spirit in seeing the connections between the Old Testament and the New Testament, or in applying the message of the Bible to their daily lives.

God's revelation to man through the sacred Scriptures is a gradual process. Just like the written word of God was prepared over a long period of time, just like awareness of the Word Incarnate continues to grow and develop in the community of the faithful, so an individual grows in an ever-expanding appreciation of the Bible when that person makes the Bible a real part of his or her life.

God's revelation to man was made complete in the life, death, and resurrection of Jesus. But, it is the Holy Spirit that continues to make the revelation clear to mankind. The Son of Man is the perfect word of God. But the full meaning of that word is comprehensible only through the advocate, the Holy Spirit, as Jesus promised his disciples at the Last Supper.

The Bible is truly a book for a lifetime. It is an endless fountain of living water. If you take a drink from that fountain only once, then walk away, never to return, then there was little value in reading it, especially if it was only done as an assignment or as a curiosity.

God's revelation is dynamic, always applicable and relevant. The understanding and appreciation that one generation may have, or the intense fervor and great spirituality that may have occurred during an awakening of some past century, may have only minimal value for today's Christians. While the burden of interpreting the Scriptures is the responsibility of the Church's Magisterium, the opportunity of finding profound spiritual fulfillment is the challenge of every person of every succeeding generation.

When someone tells me, "I have already read the entire Bible," I hope they haven't just checked off another spiritual square.

■When did the Bible Become a Book?

The earliest form of writing a "book" was the scroll, a long sheet of paper rolled up. The text was written in columns on the scroll going from left to right. The ends of a large scroll were attached to rod-like spindles to roll and unroll the paper. So, the person reading the "book" would unroll the paper in one hand and, while reading, roll it with the other hand.

The earliest material for making paper scrolls came from papyrus, a tall aquatic plant. The Egyptians invented papyrus paper using the pith from the long stalks. Strips of pith were laid out on a large surface going in one direction, and then another layer was made going crosswise. The two layers were then pressed and dried, thereby producing a good quality, inexpensive paper. Papyrus paper was usually made in rolls about nine inches wide and thirty-five feet long. The paper could be easily cut for smaller purposes, or if a larger book was needed, the papyrus rolls could be glued together.

The papyrus scroll was the common writing material in the ancient world for hundreds of years. Egypt was the main producer of papyrus, selling it to the ancient world. The Hebrews wrote their Scriptures on papyrus. Papyrus was very practical, far better than writing on clay or wooden tablets.

However, in the long run, papyrus had its shortcomings. It deteriorated in time unless it was properly stored, and even then, it couldn't last forever. Over a long period of time, it becomes brittle and frangible, and ultimately crumbles into small pieces. This is one of the reasons why no known original copies of the Hebrew Bible exist today.

Sometime during the third century B.C. a competitor in the city of Pergamen (in modern day Turkey) developed a better writing material—parchment. Parchment was made of sheep, lamb, and goat skins. The process of making parchment did not involve tanning as with leather, rather the people washed the skins, removed the hair, and soaked it in a lime solution. Then, it was stretched in a frame and scraped clean. When the skins dried, they were polished. The finished product was white and smooth, an excellent writing surface. Also, it could be written on both sides, whereas papyrus could only be written on one side. Parchment was much more durable than papyrus. It was also more expensive, so because of the cost of making parchment, papyrus continued being the preferred writing surface for several more centuries. Later parchment took over for nearly a thousand years until wood pulp paper came to the Western world.

In the early Christian era, another invention made a lasting contribution to the world of writing. Someone discovered that numerous sheets of papyrus or parchment could be folded together, thus making a book with pages. Turning pages was easier to read than unrolling a scroll. The book with pages was called a "codex."

So pages printed with front and back finally became the norm. The combination of durability of parchment and pages printable on both sides was most fortuitous for the Old and New Testaments. Early Christians copied the Holy Scriptures in codex form. Today, many of these valuable old Greek codices still exist in libraries and museums around the world. The most famous of the codices are the *Codex Alexandrinus, Codex Bezae, Codex Claramontanus, Codex Ephraemi, Codex Sinaiticus*, and *Codex Vaticanus*. The *Codex Alexandrinus* and *Codex Sinaiticus* are in the British Museum. The *Codex Ephraemi* and *Codex Claramontanus* are in the Paris National Library. The *Codex Bezae* is at Cambridge University. The *Codex Vaticanus* is in the Vatican Library.

Finally, the last big step in making the Bible into a book took place in Mainz, Germany, in 1452, when Johann Gutenberg, who invented the moveable type printing press, delivered his first book, the Latin Vulgate Bible.

■ How was the Bible written?

The first obvious point is that the Bible was written over a very long period of time. The historical narrative of the Bible covers a period of nearly two thousand years, from the story of Abraham to the development and spread of the early Christian church. Another point to consider is that the complete Bible that we have today, with the Old Testament of forty-six books (or thirty-nine in Protestant bibles), and the New Testament of twenty-seven books, was not put together into a single book until probably in the third or fourth century.

How the Bible was written is a controversial subject among Christian denominations. The Catholic Church espouses an open approach to the subject. For the Catholic Church, the matter is subject to historical scrutiny, scientific investigation and theory, literary analysis, and comparative linguistic study.

The question of how the Bible was written, focuses mostly on the Old Testament, mainly because it covers such a large period of time and because it deals with events long before the Hebrew language had developed a written form. The Old Testament deals with times that do not have clear and substantiating historical evidence of the events that happened and the personalities who lived at the time. For hundreds of years, the stories of the Hebrew people were transmitted by storytellers whose task was to hand down through each generation the beliefs and history of their people. Without writing, oral transmission was the only way to preserve the people's heritage. When a written form was finally developed, these various oral presentations, or oral traditions, were committed to writing. Because of the lack of easy communication across time and geographical distances, numerous traditions developed in various parts of the territory where the early Hebrew people lived. Biblical studies and "biblical criticism" have identified various sources of teachings and traditions that clearly illustrate that the books of the Bible were not all written, as is frequently accepted, by the person whose name is on the book.

An accepted view is that the writing of the Hebrew Scriptures began during the reign of King David around 1000 B.C., at a time when the monarchy was firmly established. In an effort to preserve the religious and historical heritage, a group of people was assigned the task of gathering all the available material and sources of the story dealing with the Hebrew people. Oral traditions, songs and hymns, genealogies, census counts, battle stories, legends, religious teachings, lists of laws and regulations, annals of various sorts were written and compiled. The group or groups responsible for this task compiled and committed to writing various sources and traditions. The formation of the written Bible had begun.

For several hundred years after this initial gathering of information and sources, the priestly authorities, scribes, and other teachers of the Hebrew community, reviewed, refined, and edited the sources and gradually combined them into the collection that we have today. This final edit of the Old Testament probably occurred somewhere around the fifth century B.C., near the time of Ezra and Nehemiah.

So, what is our answer to the question "How was the Bible written?" As far as the Old Testament is concerned, many people had a hand in creating the Bible; certainly a lot more than the twenty-five or thirty individuals that are customarily assigned to the books. Historical investigation and literary analysis have demonstrated that even well-known prophets like Isaiah, Jeremiah, Ezekiel, and Daniel have portions that could not have been written by them.

The New Testament is more cohesive than the Old Testament in its origins for several reasons. The twenty-seven books that comprise the New Testament were created within a span of seventy or eighty years. The New Testament books focus on Jesus Christ: his actions, his teaching, and the spreading of his message to all peoples. But the New Testament is also the subject of investigative scrutiny. With some exceptions, the authorship of the Epistles does not generate much diversity of opinion, because they deal more with instruction and teaching. The Gospels, however, present a different situation. Four Gospels are recognized as truly inspired by the Holy Spirit and they belong to the Canon. Even so, the Catholic Church recognizes that there are historical aspects of the Gospels that are valid subjects for deeper study and scientific investigation. The Catholic Church's Pontifical Biblical Commission in 1964 issued a paper that opened to Catholic Bible scholars the issue of the historical accuracy of the Gospels in reporting the words and deeds of Jesus. The Commission clearly expressed the idea to Catholics that the Gospels are not literal, chronological accounts of the words and deeds of Jesus Christ. Rather, our present gospels are the results of development, revision, and consolidation of sources of the life and teachings of Jesus as proclaimed through the apostles and followers in the early church.

The Catholic Church's position on the questions about how the Bible was written and who the individuals were that authored the texts is that these questions and others are open for scholarly study.

But with all the possibilities that biblical studies and biblical criticism have opened up, one belief remains undiluted: the Holy Spirit was involved and guided all those persons whose hands and minds and talents participated in creating the written word of God. And, as the Holy Spirit formed and directed the beautiful opus of the sacred Scriptures, the Holy Spirit continues throughout all times actively influencing the People of God in its understanding of what the written word is saying to every generation.

■A Reflection on Love in the Bible

As we have come through this book on Bible appreciation, we saw in an earlier section the question "What is the Bible in 25 words or less?" My answer was this: "The Bible is a written record of God's efforts to communicate with man and man's response to God. It is a love story." For the person who takes it literally to mean exactly that, the Bible is a beautiful companion to life. And, that is what it is meant to be. A companion, not a torturer of the soul and spirit.

Another section we have explored is "God of Justice, God of Love" where, I hope, we clearly established that in the Old Testament God was truly a God of love, steadfast love, a love that never fades, a perfect divine love. Much more than a God of Justice.

We've taken care of that Old Testament dilemma. Now it is time to look at the New Testament. Each of the Gospels has something to say about love.

Matthew quotes Jesus telling the young lawyer **"You shall love the Lord your God with all your heart and with all your soul and with all your mind."** This was the first and great commandment of the Old Testament (Dt.6:4-5). The second commandment **"You shall love your neighbor as yourself,"** was a New Testament addition expanding the scope of love.

Mark says the same. Luke says the same. In a different scenario, found in Matthew and Luke, **"I say to you, love your enemies and pray for those who persecute you, so that you may be sons of your father who is in heaven."** When you honestly love your enemies, this is pure love. "For if you love those who love you, what reward have you? Do not even the tax collectors do the same? And, if you salute only your brethren, what more are you doing than others? Do not even the Gentiles do the same? You, therefore, must be perfect as your heavenly father is perfect."

The three synoptics are in agreement regarding love of neighbor. Jesus was the epitome of love in his actions and the supreme forgiveness on the cross.

St. Paul in chapter 13 of his epistle to the Corinthians, penned one of the most beautiful descriptions and explanations of what love is for us. **"If I speak in tongues of men and of angels, but have not love, I am a noisy gong or a clanging cymbal. And if I have prophetic powers, and understand all mysteries and all knowledge, and if I have all faith so as to remove mountains, but have not love, I am nothing."** He enumerated the characteristics of love: patience and kindness; not jealous or boastful, arrogant or rude; it does not insist on its own way, is not irritable or resentful. Love bears all things, believes all things, hopes all things, and endures all things. These are the qualities our human love should have.

John, however, goes for beyond the synoptics and Paul's epistles. He goes into the profound theology of God's love. **"God so loved the world that he gave his only son, that whoever believes in him should not perish but have eternal life."** What intensity of God's infinite love! At the last supper, Jesus gave his discourse on love to the disciples. **"A new commandment I give to you, that you love one another; even as I have loved you, that you also love one another. By this all men will know that you are my disciples, if you have love for one another."** Jesus is love. He is the model. He doesn't say that directly, but he is getting there. **"He who loves me will be loved by my Father, and I will love him and manifest myself to him." "As the Father has loved me, so have I loved you; abide in my love."** It gets deeper: Jesus is bringing the Father into the picture. Again Jesus doesn't reveal he is divine love, but he makes another step toward it. **"This is my commandment, that you love one another as I have loved you. Greater love has no man than this that man lay down his life for his friends."** The message is for the apostles, for you and me, and for everyone, to "love one another as I have loved you." And, with this love what will happen next? **"If a man loves me, he will keep my word, and my Father will love him, and we will come to him and make our home with him."** And "we" will come? What is Jesus implying? The Father and the Son will make their home in him. God will dwell in that one. What exactly does that mean? In what way can God dwell in someone?

At this we point, we need to go to the first epistle of John to make the next big jump in understanding what the dwelling of God means. **"See what love the Father has given us, that we should be called children of God; and so we are."** And what more? **"We know you**

believe the love God has for us." Finally, we have come to the answer. In the Old Testament, God's love was steadfast love. It extended beyond just the Israelites: it extended to all things created. "For thou lovest all things that exist, and hast loathing for none of the things which thou hast made, for thou wouldst not have made anything if thou hadst hated it" (Wis 11:23–26) Now we know: God loves! It's steadfast love! God was truly a God of love in the Old Testament. His love was wonderful. It never failed. It never faded away. That was forever.

Now, with the epistle of John, we understand steadfast love completely. Steadfast love was not something God gave, because God is love. **"God is love, and he who abides in love abides in God, and God abides in him."** Translating this verse in non-biblical terms is this: "Love is so divine that we can say not only 'God is love' but 'Love is God.' Wherever there is some element of pure love—even where men do not know God—God lives there and divine life."

[The New Catechism, pg. 302, Herder and Herder, New York, 1967]

In BA, the Old Testament and the New Testament come together completely. The Bible is a book of many different books all contributing to one message. "The Bible is a written record of God's efforts to communicate with man and man's response to God. It is a love story."

The Finish Line

Congratulations! You have reached the end of *Bible Appreciation for Catholics*. Hopefully, you discovered how to navigate through the sacred Scriptures, learned things about the Bible you didn't know, and enjoyed doing it.

The Bible is a treasure chest close at hand. It's all yours...to keep forever....So, go for it!

Learn the Bible.

Love the Bible.

Live the Bible.

Appendix A: Answers to the Quizzes

Bible Appreciation Quiz for Chapter III: What do you know about the Bible?

(1.) How many books are in the Bible? 42, **66 P** and **72 C**, 84, 109 (this is a tricky question**!) It depends on whether the version is P (Protestant) or C (Catholic).**

(2.) Who were Adam and Eve's two sons? **Cain and Abel.**

(3.) Name the four Gospels. **Matthew, Mark, Luke, John.**

(4.) What is the first book of the Bible? **Genesis.**

(5.) Was Abraham's wife turned into a pillar of salt? **No, it was Lot's wife.**

(6.) King David was the father of which Israelite king? **Solomon.**

(7.) What book of the Bible records the events of Moses bringing the Israelites out of Egypt? **Exodus.**

(8.) Which of the following titles is not a book of the Bible? **Joshua, Isaiah, Moses, Daniel, Numbers.**

(9.) Abraham lived about 1900 B.C. Calculating the genealogies according to the Bible, when did Adam live? **500 B.C.; 4000 B.C.; 10,000 B.C.; 20,000 B.C.**

(10.) What is the last book of the Bible? **Revelations.**

(11.) What is the Pentateuch? **The first 5 books of the Bible.**

(12.) How many epistles of St. Peter are there in the Bible? **Two**

(13.) What book of the Bible talks about "Vanity of vanities, all is vanity?" **Ecclesiastes**

(14.) Name the four major prophets of the Old Testament. **Isaiah, Jeremiah, Ezekiel, Daniel.**

(15.) Name three Judges of the Old Testament.
These are the names of the judges: Othniel, Ehud, Shamgar, Deborah, Barak, Gideon, Tola, Jair, Jephthah, Ibzan, Elon, Abdon, and Samson.

(16.) What is a deuterocanonical book of the Bible and why is it important?

The deuterocanonical books of the Bible were those books that were included in the Septuagint. The deuterocanonical books of the Bible were part of the Canon that was decreed in the Council of Trent.

(17.) What is Bible "pre-history" and what is its all important message?

Genesis, Chapters 1–11 are not considered historical. They are called "pre-history." The message is important as the stories teach universal truths.

(18.) Where in the Bible do we find the names of the twelve apostles?

Mt. 10:1–14; Mk 3:13–19; Lk 6:12–16.

See if you can find…

(1.) The story of the Tower of Babel – **Gen 10:10–11:9**.

(2.) When was Daniel thrown into the lion's den – **Dan 6:17–25**

(3.) When seven brothers offered themselves in martyrdom – **2 Mac 7:1–42.**

(4.) When Jacob got Esau's birth right – **Gen 25:32 and 27:36.**

(5.) When Samson had his long hair cut off – **Jg 16:16–21.**

(6.) The walls of Jericho collapse – **Jos 6:1–20.**

(7.) When Moses received the Ten Commandments – **Ex 20:1–17**

(8.) The story of Jezebel and all her wicked deeds – **1 Kg 18–19.**

(9.) When Elijah walked forty days – **2 Kg 19:1–8.**

(10.) When Jacob was tricked by Laban to work seven extra years – **Gen 29:14–30**

(11.) The last king of Judah is blinded and taken into captivity – **2 Kg 25:1–7.**

(12.) Which Psalm says that a person that "meditates on the Law of the Lord day and night is like a tree rooted near streams of water" – **Ps 1.**

(13.) Where do we find the story of the great-grandmother of King David – **Ruth 1–4.**

(14.) When the angel changed Jacob's name to Israel – **Gen 32:22–28.**

(15.) When the prophet was swallowed by a giant fish (or whale) – **Jon 1:1–16 to 2:11.**

(16.) Where is the famous verse "For everything there is a season…A time to live and a time to die, a time to sow and a time to reap – **Ecc 3:1–8.**

(1.) How many gospels are considered "synoptic?" **Three: Matthew, Mark, and Luke.**

(2.) Where do you go to find the eight beatitudes? **Matthew.**

(3.) Which gospel used a genealogy to demonstrate that Jesus was truly the Royal lineage? **Matthew**

(4.) In what gospel do you find the miracle of the multiplication of bread? **Matthew, Mark, Luke, John. This is the only miracle of Jesus recorded in all four gospels: Mt 14:13–21; Mk 6:32–44; Lk 9:10–17; Jn 6: 4–13**

(5.) Which gospel reports Jesus bringing a dead man back to life? **John, when Jesus was in Bethany**

(6.) Which evangelist wrote about the miracle of changing water into wine? **John, 2:1–11**

(7.) Was Matthew the evangelist who wrote for an audience of Gentile Christians? **No. There were two, Mark and Luke.**

(8.) How many journeys of St. Paul are recorded in the Acts of the Apostles? **Three (3)**

Can you match prophet and prophecy?

(1.) "There shall come forth a shoot from the stump of Jesse, a branch will grow from the root, and the spirit of the Lord shall rest upon him, the spirit of wisdom and understanding...." **Isaiah 11:1**

(2.) "They shall beat their swords into ploughshares, and their spears into pruning hooks; nation shall not lift up sword against nation, neither shall they learn war any more." **Isaiah 2:4 and Micah 4:3**

(3.) "You, Bethlehem of Ephrata, you are the littlest of the clans of Judah. Out of you will come forth the ruler of Israel and his going forth shall be from eternity." **Micah 5:2**

(4.) "A time is coming, says the Lord, when I will make a new covenant with the house of Israel and the house of Judah. It will not be like the old covenant I made with their forefathers...." **Jeremiah 31:31–32**

(5.) "The spirit of the Lord is upon me. He has sent me to proclaim the good news to the poor, to set captives free...." **Isaiah 61:1**

(6.) "Behold, a virgin shall conceive and bear a son, and his name shall be called Emmanuel." **Isaiah 7:14**

(7.) Who interpreted for King Belshazzar the message *"mene, mene, teqel, parqin"* that a hand wrote on the wall? **Daniel 5:25–28**

(1.) Does the Catholic Church teach that the Bible was dictated by God? **No.**

(2.) Does the Catholic Church teach that the Bible is the inspired word of God? **Yes**

(3.) Why was there a Greek translation of the Hebrew Bible? **Because the Jews of the diaspora spoke Greek, and wanted a Bible they could read and understand.**

(4.) What is meant by the Canon of the New Testament? **The Canon was the recognized list of authentic scriptures in the Christian world.**

(5.) What was the name given to the Greek translation of the Hebrew Bible? **Septuagint**

(6.) Does the Catholic Church teach that the human writers of the Bible were in a trance? **No.**

(7.) What do you understand about the meaning of the parade? **This is my understanding. The history of salvation and God's faithfulness and love, from the pre-history prologue to the Apocalypse epilogue. What did you understand?**

(1.) What is meant by "the word of God in the words of men?" **That God's infallible message and revelations were written by men in the language they knew and the circumstances that surrounded them.**

(2.) Where do they keep the original manuscript of the Old Testament? **There is no known original manuscript.**

(3.) What is the holistic approach to the Bible? **To see and read it from the "big picture," and to understand the profound message gives it us.**

(4.) What is meant by "pre-history" in the Bible? **A time that does not meet the criteria of historicity: identifiable time and place.**

(5.) What are two divine attributes of God ? **Eternal and immutable are the two mentioned. Other attributes are omnipotent, omniscient, infinite, omnipresent.**

(6.) What is the difference between Apocalypse and Apocrypha? **Apocalypse (John's Revelations) and Apocrypha (books not found the Palestine Canon, but are listed in the Alexandrian Canon).**

(7.) When did the Catholic Church officially define the Christian Canon of the Bible? **In the Council of Trent, during its Fourth Session (1546).**

What do you know about the Catholic Church Teaching on the Bible?

(1.) When did Pope Benedict XIII promulgate his encyclical on the Bible, *Providentissimus Deus*? **1893.**

(2.) What is the name of the document of Vatican II that explains doctrine of the Bible? **Dogmatic Constitution on Divine Revelation**

(3.) What is the title of Pope Benedict XVI's Apostolic Exhortation on the Holy Scriptures? **Verbum Domini**

(4.) What are the three categories of biblical interpretation? **The literal sense, the spiritual sense, and the fuller sense**

(5.) What is the *Magisterium* of the Catholic Church? **The *Magisterium* refers to the teaching authority of the church.**

(6.) What does the term "deuterocanonical" refer to? **A group of sacred books listed on the Catholic biblical canon that are not accepted in the Hebrew Bible and Protestant Bible.**

(7.) What is the Protestant term for "deuterocanonical?" **The Catholic deuterocanonical books are called Apocrypha.**

What do you know about women in the Old Testament?

Eve, Gen 2–7, **The first woman mentioned in the Bible and wife of Adam.**

Adah, Gen 4:20, **One of the two wives of Lamech.**

Bilhah, Gen 29–30; 37, **A maid of Rebecca and mother of two sons, Dan and Naphtali.**

Zipporah, Ex 2; 4, **Wife of Moses and mother of two sons, Gershom and Eliezer.**

Sarah, Gen 12–15, **Wife of Abraham and the mother of Isaac.**

Leah, Gen 29–35, **Wife of Jacob and older sister of Rachel, and mother of six sons: Ruben, Simeon, Levi, Judah, Issachar, and Zebulun.**

Miriam, Ex 15, **Prophetess and sister to Aaron.**

Rebecca, Gen 24–27, **Wife of Isaac and mother of Esau and Jacob.**

Zilpah, Gen 30; 35, **Leah's maid who gave birth to Gad and Asher.**

Zillah, Gen 4:20, **Second wife of Lamech,**

Jochebed, Nb 26, **Daughter of Levi and mother of Aaron and Moses.**

Rachel, Gen 29–35, **Wife of Jacob and mother of**

Joseph and Benjamin.

Asenath, Gen 41: 46, **Wife of Joseph and mother of Manasseh and Ephraim.**

Ruth, Rt 1–**4, Great-grandmother of King David.**

Bible Appreciation Quiz for Chapter IX– Women 2

How many women of the Old Testament are you familiar with?

Rahah, Jos 2, **6, Prostitute who assisted Israelite spies going to the promised land.**

Abigail, 1 Sam 25, 27, **Wife of King David.**

Deborah, Jg 4–5, **Prophet this during the time of the judges.**

Bathsheba, 2 Sam 11–12, **Wife of Uriah, the man David sent to be killed so he could have Bathsheba as his wife.**

Delilah, Jg 16, **Seduced Samson and cut off his long hair, his source of strength.**

Jezebel, 1 Kg 16–21, **Seductress and evil queen in the time of the prophet Elijah.**

Hannah, 1 Sam 1–2, **Wife of Elkanah, and mother of Samuel.**

Judith, Book of Judith, **Heroine who saved the Israelite, decapitating the enemy general.**

Ahinoam, 1 Sam 25, 27, **Wife of King David**

Esther, Est 1–10 **Beautiful Jewish women who became queen and saved her people**.

Bible Appreciation Quiz for Chapter IX – Women 3

How many women of the New Testament are you familiar with?

Anna, who was she? **Lk 2, A holy prophetess at the time of Jesus's infancy.**

Apphia, who was she? **Ph 1, Mentioned as a worker for Christ with Philemon.**

Bernice, who was she? **Act 25 , The sister of Herod Agrippa**

Chloe, who was she? **1 Cor 1, A woman who Paul mentioned for her help in Corinth.**

Claudia, who was she? **2 Tim 4, A Christian woman mentioned in Paul's letter.**

Dorcas, who was she? **Act 9, A different name for Tabitha, the one Peter raided from the dead.**

Elizabeth, who was she? **Lk 1, A cousin of Mary, and mother of John the Baptist.**

Joanna, who was she? **Lk 24, A woman who was with Mary Magdalene at the tomb on Easter Sunday morning**

Lydia, who was she? **Act 16, A hospitable woman who had invited apostles in her house.**

Herodias, who was she? **Mt 14; Mk 6, Wife of King Herod who asked for John the Baptist's head**

Mary, Mother of Jesus **Lk 1, (everyone knows her)**

Mary Magdalene **Jn 19; Lk 8; Mk 15; Mt 27, A follower of Jesus.**

Mary, who was she? **Mk 15, The mother of James and Joses, and Salome.**

Martha, who was she? **Jn 11, A friend of Jesus and sister of Mary and Lazarus.**

Prisca, who was she? **Act 18, Also known as Priscilla, wife of Aquila, helper in Christian community of Corinth.**

Salome, who was she? **Mk 15 , A young woman, follower of Jesus, present at the Crucifixion.**

Sapphira, who was she? **Act 5, The wife of Ananias died for lying to Peter about money.**

Tabitha, who was she? **Act 9, The young woman Peter raised from the dead.**

Tryphaena, who was she? **Rm 16, Mentioned as woman who was a worker in the Lord.**

Tryphosa, who was she? **Rm 16, Mentioned as a woman who was a worker in the Lord.**

Appendix B: God's Steadfast love

A list of Old Testament passages that speak of God's steadfast love (or faithful love, everlasting love, or mercy, depending on the translation).

From the Historical Books

Genesis, chapter 24 verse 12; chapter 32:10; and 39:10.

Exodus, chapter 34:7.

Deuteronomy, chapter 5:10; 7:9; 7:12.

2 Samuel, chapter 8:15; 15:20.

1 Kings, chapter 8:23.

2 Chronicles, chapter 5:23; 6:14; 6:42; 7:3; 7:6; 20:31.

Ezra, chapter 3:11; 7:28; 9:9.

Nehemiah, chapter 1:5.

From the prophets

Isaiah, chapter 54:8–10; 55:10; 56:3; 63:7

Jeremiah, 33:10; 9:24; 16:5; 32:18; 31:3.

Lamentations, chapter 3:32.

Daniel, chapter 9:4

Hosea, chapter 2:21; 6:6; 11:12.

Joel, chapter 2:13

Micah, chapter 7:20

Jonah, chapter 4:2

Zephaniah, chapter 3:7

From the books of Wisdom

Wisdom, chapter 12:24

Job, chapter 10:12

From the book of Psalms

Forty-seven psalms speak of God's steadfast love/faithful love/ everlasting love

Psalm 5, 17, 18, 21, 25, 26, 31, 32, 33, 36, 40, 43, 44, 48, 51, 52, 57, 59, 61, 62, 63, 66, 69, 77, 85, 86, 88, 89, 90, 92, 93, 100, 103, 106, 107, 108, 109, 115, 117, 118, 119, 130, 136, 138, 143, 145, 147

Glossary

A.D. — Era *Anno Domini*, Latin, meaning "Year of the Lord."

apocalyptic — Term given to writings that claim to be from divine revelations

Apocrypha — Name given to a group of books in the Bible that have dubious authenticity.

Aramaic — Middle-eastern language that replaced the Hebrew language as a common tongue during the post-exilic period and during the early years of Christianity.

Assyria — Ancient Mesopotamian empire that dominated the region for about 400 years, and conquered the Northern Kingdom of Israel in 722 B.C.

Babylon — Ancient Mesopotamian empire that dominated the region several different times and conquered the Southern Kingdom of Judah in 587 B.C.

B.C. — Era Before Christ

Canon — List of authentically approved documents or information. The term is used for both the Old and New Testaments.

creationism — As Religious Creationism, professes the creation of world as we see it is exactly as described in the Bible. It rejects evolution in the development of the world.

deuterocanonical — Designation of a group of biblical books that were not listed in the Hebrew Canon. Deuterocanonical is a Catholic term. Protestant Bibles list as Apocrypha.

Dei Verbum — Latin, meaning Word of God.

Diaspora — The dispersion of the Hebrews.

Divino Afflante Spiritu — Latin title for the encyclical of Pope XII. The English title is "Inspired by the Holy Spirit."

Dogmatic Constitution — A major presentation of the Church's beliefs.

Fundamentalism — A movement in Protestantism begun in the United States that emphasizes the inerrancy and literal meaning of the Bible.

genre — A type or style of something, usually applied to literature and the arts.

Hellenistic — The spread of the Greek culture following the time and conquest of Alexander the Great.

inerrancy — Free from error.

Holistic — Term used to describe the complete, wholeness view of a subject

lectionary — An organized selection of readings from the Bible.

Magisterium — The teaching authority of the Catholic Church

Northern Kingdom — One of two parts of the division of the Hebrew Monarchy following the death of King Solomon. It was known as Israel.

Pentateuch — Name of the group of the first five books of the Greek translation of the Bible.

Persia — Empire in southwestern Asia that dominated the region during the sixth, fifth, and fourth centuries B.C.

post-exilic — Term used to describe the historical period of the Jewish people after their return from the Babylonian captivity.

pre-exilic — Term used to describe the historical period of the Jewish people before their Babylonian captivity.

pre-history — Term used to describe the world of mankind in the book of Genesis , Chapters 1–11.

Providentissimus Deus — Latin for the Most Provident God.

Southern Kingdom — One of two parts of the division of the Hebrew Monarchy following the death of King Solomon. It was known as Judah.

Septuagint — The Greek translation of the Bible generated by the Jewish people of the diaspora

Torah — The first five books of the Hebrew Sacred Scriptures, meaning "The Law."

Trent, Council of — The ecumenical council convened by the Catholic Church in 1545.

Vatican I — The ecumenical council convened by the Catholic Church, 1869–70.

Vatican II — The ecumenical council convened by the Catholic Church, 1961–1965.

General Bibliography

Bible

New Catholic Study Bible, St. Jerome Edition, Catholic Bible Press, 1985.

New English Bible, New Testament, Oxford University Press and Cambridge University Press, 1961.

New Jerusalem Bible (English), Doubleday, New York, 1990, ISBN 0-385-14264-1.

New Oxford Annotated Bible with the Apocrypha (Revised Standard Version), Oxford University Press, New York, 1973, Library of Congress CCN: 76-42682.

Novi Testamenti Biblia Graeca et Latina, (edidit, Joseph M. Boyer, S.I) Editio Quarta, Madrid, 1959.

Old Testament (translated from the Vulgate Latin, by Msgr. Ronald Knox), Vol I and II, Sheed & Ward, Inc., New York, 1952.

One Year Bible (New Revised Standard Version)World Bible Publishers, Inc., Iowa Falls, Iowa, 1991, and Tyndale House Publishers, Inc., Wheaton, Illinois, ISBN 0-8423-4744-5.

Encyclopedias and Encyclopedic Dictionaries

Cruden, Alexander. *Cruden's Complete Concordance* (edited by A.D. Adams, C.H. Irwin, S.A. Waters), Hold, Rinehart and Winston, New York, 1949.

McKenzie, John L., S. J. *Dictionary of the Bible.* The Bruce Publishing Company, Milwaukee, 1965, Library of Congress CCN: 65-26691.

Rahner, Karl, and Herbert Vorgrimler, *Theological Dictionary.* Herder and Herder, New York, 1965, Library of Congress CCN: 65-26562.

The Church Teaches — Documents of the Church in English Translation, B. Herder Book Co., St. Louis, 1955, Library of Congress CCN:55-10397.

Biblical Studies

A Catholic Commentary on Holy Scripture, Thomas Nelson & Sons, New York, 1953. Library of Congress CCN: 53-9447.

Beal, Timothy. *Bible Literacy.* Harper One, New York, 2009. ISBN 978-0-06-171862-5.

Fee, Gordon D., and Douglas Stuart. *How to Read the Bible Book by Book.* Zondervan, Grand Rapids, MI, 2002. ISBN 0-310-21118-2.

Peake, Arthur S. *The Bible, Its Origin, Its Significance, and Its Abiding Worth.* Hodder and Stoughton, New York and London, 1913.

Perkins, Pheme. *Reading the New Testament — An Introduction.* Paulist Press, New York, 1977. ISBN 0-8091-9535-6.

Stedman, Ray C. *Adventuring through the Bible*. Discovery House Publishers, Grand Rapids, MI, 1996. ISBN 0-929239-98-9.

Wikenhauser, Alfred. *New Testament Introduction*. Herder and Herder, 1963. Library of Congress CCN: 58-5870.

Biblical Histories

Coogan, Michael D. *Oxford History of the Biblical World.* Oxford University Press, New York, 1998. ISBN 0-19-508707-0.

De Hamel, Christopher. *The Book. A History of the Bible*. Phaidon Press Ltd, London, 2001. IBSN 0 7148 3774 1.

Heinich, Paul, and William G. Heidt. *History of the Old Testament.* The Liturgical Press, Collegeville, MN, 1952.

Lampe, G.W.H. (ed.). *Cambridge History of the Bible*. Cambridge University Press, London, 1969. Library of Congress Catalog Number; 63-24435.

Catholic Dogma and Teachings

Clarkson, S.J., John H. Edwards; William J. Kelly, S.J.; John J. Welch, S.J. *The Church Teaches*. B. Herder Book Co, St. Louis, 1955. Library of Congress CCN: 55-10397.

Ott, Ludwig B. *Fundamentals of Catholic Dogma*. Herder Book Co., St. Louis, 1955.

Post-Synodal Apostolic Exhortation of the Holy Father Benedict XVI, Rome, 2010.

Other Books

Callahan, Tim. *Secret Origins of the Bible.* Millennium Press, Altadena, California, 2002. ISBN: 0-965-5047-8-6.

Sheeler, Jeffrey L. *Is the Bible True.* Harper San Francisco, 1999. ISBN 0-06-067541-1.

White, James R. *Scripture Alone.* Bethany House, Minneapolis, 2004. ISBN 0-7642-2048-9.

Internet Sources

Catholic Church Documents related to Biblical Studies, compiled by Felix Just, S.J., http://myweb.lmu.edu/fjust/ChurchDocs.htm

Documents of the Ecumenical Councils

Excerpts from the Catechism of the Catholic Church

Papal Documents

Documents of the Pontifical Biblical Commission

Neo-Vulgate Bible

Other (related) Documents

Printed collections of Church Documents

Index

D

David, 53, 54, 73, 137

Dei Verbum vi, 110, 182

Deuterocanonical vii, 122, 123, 182

diaspora 172, 183

E

epistle 87, 103, 160, 161, 162

Eucharist, 16

F

Fundamentalism 84, 101, 182

G

genre 82, 118, 182

gospel, 75, 77, 94

Greek language, 89

H

Hebrew language 24, 88, 89, 157, 181

Holistic vi, 99, 182

I

inerrancy, 121

inspiration, 63, 83, 122

L

lectio divina 114, 115

lectionary 182

CPSIA information can be obtained at www.ICGtesting.com
Printed in the USA
BVOW030440111212

307781BV00002B/2/P